Words of Endearment

The Ten Commandments As a Revelation of God's Love

Dr. William B. Coker, Sr.

Sermon To Book
www.sermontobook.com

Words of Endearment / Dr. William B. Coker, Sr.
ISBN-13: 978-1-952602-13-9

To all the people
who have grown spiritually
because of God's call upon my life
to reveal His truth
through teaching and preaching
in classrooms, churches,
and on mission fields.

Ann L. Coker

In an age of secularism, godlessness, inner city violence and turmoil, police brutality, and general disregard for law and order in the name of protest and free speech, this book answers the call for a return to the Ten Commandments and the benevolent rule of God in the hearts and minds of His people. There is no cure for the cultural disintegration around us without addressing the urgent need to restore respect for God's Law as an expression of His love and His road map, not only for personal holiness, but for a just and peaceful society in which to live. This is Dr. Coker's crowning achievement of a lifetime of study and dedication to spreading the Good News of the gospel, and in this case, the Ten Commandments as the road map to a peaceful and just society. Whether you are a Christian or not, this book will open your eyes to the "Ten Commandments as a revelation of God's love."

Barry Bostrom, Attorney at Law, Terre Haute, IN

For those of us who have long valued hearing the Word explicated by Dr. Bill Coker, this gem of a book powerfully communicates in new ways the importance of following God's "words of endearment" to achieve spiritual growth as a follower of Jesus Christ. The review of each "word" (commandment) is set in a clearly understood historical context, including valuable Hebrew definitions, followed by practical application for life today, all written in an engaging style. This powerful message encourages the reader to reassure that God's boundaries, established because of His love for us, are a vital part of our daily living.

Bonnie J. Banker, Ed.D., Asbury University, retired, Wilmore, KY

A book and its author go together like a trumpet and the breath going through. One of the Hebrew symbols in the Bible for God's voice is the shofar. While reading this book I couldn't help but hear His voice through the written recording of God's shofar called Bill Coker. The breath of the Holy Spirit goes through His treasured instrument, producing an everlasting sound of His love from His fatherly heart for His children. Therefore, don't be too puzzled by the unusual shape of this book. If you listen carefully, you may hear God's voice, too, maybe even for the first time!

Dr. Stefanie Gutschmidt, Associate Professor in Mechanical Engineering, University of Canterbury, Christchurch, New Zealand

Just as the years I sat under Pastor Bill's preaching, teaching, and pastoral prayers enriched my spiritual growth, his words in print challenge and inspire in me a desire to live a life that pleases and glorifies God. There is not one page of this book that does not contain words of significant value for a life lived worshiping the Great I AM. Do my actions in life proclaim the One True God? Or do my actions show a lack of reverence for the power of His name? Pastor Bill points out that of all the tasks we are given to do on earth, worship is the one thing that remains eternal. Praise to our God Most High!

Sally Wire, member of World Gospel Church, Terre Haute, IN

To be a pastor, you must be a teacher. If you are a pastor and not a teacher, you are an entertainer. Dr. Coker is a pastor with the heart of a teacher. Dr. Coker starts the reader off with the understanding that the "Ten Words" are for the purpose of a joyful life and a loving relationship with our Father. He then ends with a call for each of us to have a God-centered purpose in our lives, and to reach out to others so that they, too, can attain that goal. This book is for new Christians who want to learn what the real responsibilities of Christian life are, and for old and "wise" Christians who may need to be reminded.

Paul Zurcher, Pastor of Croy's Creek Congregational Christian Church, Poland, IN

As a former student, and a ministry teammate, I experienced Dr. Coker's depth of teaching and preaching God's Word. Here in his book, he has presented the Word of God in such a dynamic and inspiring way that readers are deeply blessed and inspired. I do not believe a deeper understanding of God's ten "words of endearment" (the Ten Commandments) can be found elsewhere. We often simplify what we know about the commandments of God by seeing them as rules to follow. But the depth of understanding presented in this book will inspire you to live above the level of normal human response to these guidelines for living. God's "words of endearment" need to affect our individual lives, our families, our church families, our communities, and even our nation.

Rev. Charles Jones, Sr., Evangelist and Minister of Music, Albany, GA

Readers will find here a thorough knowledge of the historical background of the Decalogue, of the distinctive linguistic issues in them, of their significance to the Hebrew people, and of their abiding relevance to all humanity, including us today. While the commands are pronouncements from "on high," Dr. Coker's expositions are not. They are thoughtful, well-informed reflections from a brother on the way. As Dr. Coker maintains, these ten "words," as the Jewish people have designated them, are not the demands of a heavenly tyrant, which we disobey at our own peril. They are directions from the Creator, given to us in love.

Dr. John N. Oswalt, Old Testament Scholar, Wilmore, KY (from Foreword)

What a privilege and joy to write an endorsement of Dr. Bill Coker's *Words of Endearment: The Ten Commandments As a Revelation of God's Love*. With his characteristic depth of insight and straightforward communication, Dr. Coker helps us to understand the Ten Commandments as a photo of who God is. He shows us how this revelation to the people of Israel was intended by God to draw them into a personal relationship with Him, where they received blessings and boundaries. Pastor Bill then accurately and convincingly shows that this is exactly what God desires for us today. God desires us to have an intimate relationship with Him that will bring blessing and provide boundaries for daily living. The discussion/reflection questions at the end of each chapter are extremely helpful for us, as the readers, to work through the application of these words of endearment in our own lives today.

Rev. Dr. William H. Vermillion, Canby, OR, Theological Leadership Education and Discipleship Team, One Mission Society

Words of Endearment is a wonderful examination of the Decalogue from God's point of view. Each commandment given through Moses to Israel (and by extension, to all Christendom) is shown to reveal God's love for His children by setting boundaries within which all can live full and free lives in covenant with the sovereign loving God and each other. The "Words" teach us how to worship God in spirit and in truth. They teach us that we are His and He is ours. Pastor Bill's exposition is deep, yet clear, and filled with applications that help believers make proper choices, while giving us ever deepening fellowship with God. The book will become a treasure to be read and reread by Christians. It will also light the way for the unbeliever to experience the joy of salvation through Jesus Christ.

Charles Mallory North, Jr., Ph.D., Brazil, IN

Statute law in America provides its citizens with the knowledge that if you do certain acts, then you are guilty and under judgment. All too often, I view God's Commandments as the opposite: a list of strict, restrictive rules that we must do or be found guilty and under judgment. If you are like me, then Dr. Coker's *Words of Endearment* is a must-read. Instead of being another check-box list of vain requirements, Dr. Coker shows, God's commandments provide a liberating guide for how we should live, every day, in everything we do, as our response to God's love for us.

Aaron Dobrin, Patrol Officer, Lafayette, IN, Police Department

Dr. Bill Coker, "Rabbi Bill" as we affectionately call him, brings the insight and skill of a master teacher to open our eyes to the revelation of God to His people, words of guidance for relationship with God and with man. Come hear afresh these words of endearment, spoken by a loving God, illuminated by a dear teacher and friend, and launch into a more abundant experience of God.

Dr. David Prentice, Vice President and Research Director, Charlotte Lozier Institute

Bill Coker's book offers a deep and beautifully positive understanding of the Ten Commandments.

June Barrow, Assistant Pastor, First Presbyterian Church, Bonita Springs, FL

Acknowledgments

We thank first our Almighty God, who gave us His words of endearment. Our deepest gratitude goes to our family and friends who have supported us and prayed for this book project. Help with biblical languages came from our son, Rev. William B. Coker, Jr. Our daughter, Rebecca Gearhart, prepared delicious meals, making it possible for Ann to have more time at the computer. Thank you, Michael Gearhart, our grandson, for converting cassette tapes of the sermons into digital audio files. Thanks also to the skilled staff of Sermon to Book. Debbie Oliver, client success manager, and Maria Floros, chief of staff, led us through the process with good advice and kind words. Editors' notes indicated their appreciation for this pastor's message and biblical knowledge. We are especially grateful for the congregation of World Gospel Church, Terre Haute, Indiana, who heard the original messages and encouraged its publication. May God suit a blessing to each person's need.

Dr. William B. Coker, Sr. and Ann L. Coker

CONTENTS

Foreword by Dr. John N. Oswalt 3

Preface 7

The Decalogue 9

The First Word: No Other Gods 23

The Second Word: Worship Yahweh 43

The Third Word: Don't Profane My Name 67

The Fourth Word: Keep the Sabbath Day Holy 85

The Fifth Word: Honor Your Parents 105

The Sixth Word: Life Belongs to God 125

The Seventh Word: Marriage Is a Covenant 145

The Eighth Word: It All Belongs to God 167

The Ninth Word: Speak Truth 185

The Tenth Word: Desire Good Things 205

Rightly Handling the Word of Truth 225

Notes 245

About the Author 251

About Sermon To Book 253

Foreword by Dr. John N. Oswalt

When William 'Bill' Coker and I were in seminary together many years ago, I recognized a number of things about him: he had a powerful intellect, a strong work ethic, and a deep commitment to Christ. All these characteristics were focused on his determination to know and teach God's Word, the Bible.

Those characteristics guided Bill through graduate school, college professorship, college deanship, and ultimately a long and fruitful pastoral ministry. They are displayed in this volume, a collection of his sermons on the Decalogue, the Ten Commandments.

Readers will find here a thorough knowledge of the historical background of the Decalogue, of the distinctive linguistic issues in them, of their significance to the Hebrew people, and their abiding relevance to all humanity, including us today.

But Dr. Coker, giving us all these essentials, gives us more. In these discussions, there is warmth of understanding. These are not dry and dull, though comprehensive, essays. They are addresses to us, pilgrims on the way, from a fellow pilgrim. He knows our human condition and understands our questions. While the commands are pronouncements from "on high," Dr. Coker's expositions are not. They are thoughtful, well-informed reflections from a brother on the way. As such, they are welcoming, inviting us to join him in reflecting on how these all-important "words of endearment" relate to us.

As Dr. Coker maintains, these ten "words," as the Jewish people have designated them, are not the demands of a heavenly tyrant, which we disobey at our own peril. They are directions from the Creator, given to us in love. As Dr. Coker says in his introduction, the commands are boundary markers that, if we stay within them, give us full freedom to enjoy life as the Creator intended. Think, he says, what our culture, our world, would be like if, for the love of the one saving God, no one stole, or lied, or murdered, or committed adultery, or was consumed with greed to possess what another possessed. So, these are not onerous demands designed to limit our freedom. Rather, they are guides to a life of blessing and hope, the refusal of which can only lead to futility, misery, and despair.

In this book the reader will be led into a thoughtful exploration of the meaning and implications of these foundational truths by someone well-qualified by temperament, training, and experience to give that leadership. Take this journey with Bill Coker and you will have a better understanding of the boundary markers, a greater appreciation for the depth of meaning hidden in their apparent simplicity, and a renewed motivation to live within them.

Dr. John N. Oswalt
Asbury Theological Seminary
Wilmore, Kentucky

A PERSONAL NOTE

Preface

For years I have asked Bill to write a book. Others who have heard him preach and teach also encouraged him to publish his messages. He would say there are too many books in print. Then came dementia, and unfortunately, Bill is no longer able to participate in preparing or editing his sermons for publication.

It's been my dream to see my husband's sermons published. I now have the opportunity to do so. When Bill would see me with his typed sermons, he would ask what I was doing as I scribbled notes in blue ink. To avoid using the word "editing," I told him I was changing his preaching voice to a reading voice. This style did not alter Bill's messages, only prepared them for publication and you, the readers.

Bill and I hope you discover a passion for God's words of endearment and a deeper understanding of their significance. May God direct your application of His Word.

Ann L. Coker

INTRODUCTION

The Decalogue

As Christians, there are some serious questions we must address if we are going to speak about the place of the Ten Commandments in the church and in the world. First, we need to understand the meaning of the terms. In the Greek, the word for the Ten Commandments is *Decalogue,* or "ten words," which is how I will most often refer to the Ten Commandments from this point forward.

The Decalogue has to do with God's revelation of Himself to a people—originally the descendants of Abraham through his grandson Jacob (Israel) after their exodus from Egypt. As we delve deeper into this study, I want you to see the context in Scripture, to get it firmly fixed in your mind. Then, as we go forward in this book, you will have a firm understanding of where we are and the context as I am explaining these different words of endearment.

It's important to note that the Decalogue is not primarily about Israel. Rather, it represents the revelation of who

God is and has always been. Moses speaks of this in the book of Exodus:

> The LORD called to [Moses] out of the mountain, saying, "Thus you shall say to the house of Jacob, and tell the people of Israel: You yourselves have seen what I did to the Egyptians, and how I bore you on eagles' wings and brought you to myself. Now therefore, if you will indeed obey my voice and keep my covenant, you shall be my treasured possession among all peoples, for all the earth is mine; and you shall be to me a kingdom of priests and a holy nation. These are the words that you shall speak to the people of Israel."
>
> So Moses came and called the elders of the people and set before them all these words that the LORD had commanded him. All the people answered together and said, "All that the LORD has spoken we will do." And Moses reported the words of the people to the LORD.
>
> —Exodus 19:3b–8

In these words, spoken by God, notice that the context is one where God is revealing Himself to the people that He has chosen to be His. Prior to this, the people of Israel had only lived in pagan lands with pagan gods. Each of these gods had their own peculiarities in terms of character and will. There were gods for seasons, gods for specific bodies of water, and even gods who ruled over specific hills and valleys. But God revealed Himself as the One who ruled over all of creation and everything in it.

It's essential at the beginning that people understand who God is. This is the purpose of these words of the Decalogue.

In the first instance, God's words say to the people of Israel that this is the God who called you to Himself. This is the God who is giving you the opportunity to be His people, to follow His will and direction, and this is the revelation of who God is.

The Decalogue is the moral and spiritual photograph of God. It depicts who God is. They needed to know, "Who is this God before whom we bow down?" Knowing God is important, and we'll tie it all together as we move through this book.

Revealed Nature

We say that God has created the universe and that the universe bears the imprint of God who created it. That makes perfectly good sense and can be seen in human creativity.

For instance, when I create a sermon, I like to create it in such a way that is best for everybody, but it is also a reflection of me. I create something from within me, which gives anyone who listens to the sermon an idea of who I am. We also see this in art, in literature, and in music. When we create something new, we do so in such a way that it bears something of our image. Thus, the words spoken by God reveal to us the nature of God.

Words of Endearment

When we look at the ten words that make up what we call the Ten Commandments, or Decalogue, I want you to look at them as I've titled this book, *Words of Endearment*. I hope this will help you understand the Lord's words a little differently than we have understood them in the past.

In the eighteenth century, the word *endearment* came to mean "an expression of love."[1] When we come to the Decalogue, we find primarily an expression of love. When we focus on God's words as an expression of love rather than a series of obligations, our image of God goes from a wrathful deity waiting to strike hapless individuals to a Father showing His children how to live a full and abundant life, free of fear.

But in the seventeenth century, *endearment* had a different connotation. It meant "an obligation of gratitude."[2] The gift of love is received, and in response the recipient does something. That is endearment. The Jewish philosopher Martin Buber said that the Ten Commandments do not tell me what I *must* not do; they tell me what I *will* not do as a believer.[3] Your obedience to the commandments is not the means to your salvation; it is a response to God's grace and His love for you.

The reason I prefer the word *endearment* to the word *commandment* is because commands are often viewed as a form of oppression or military might. As a result, we tend to think of God demanding and booming a list of rules at Moses. This creates a wrong image of God. If we look at a parallel passage in Deuteronomy 6, God's intention and words are made clear.

> And the LORD commanded us to do all these statutes, to fear
> [reverence] the LORD our God, for our good always, that he
> might preserve us alive, as we are this day.
> **—Deuteronomy 6:24**

If that is the case, what is the intent of these ten words of endearment? In Deuteronomy 6:24, Moses said God's statutes are for our good. God has given us these words *not* because He is sitting up on the mountain saying, "I'm God, and just to remind you, I am giving you these commandments and you'd better not disobey Me—or else."

In John 3:17, Jesus said He had not come to judge the world, but to save the world. Later He said, "I came that they may have life and have it abundantly" (John 10:10).

When I look at the Decalogue, I understand what God is primarily saying to the people of Israel (and as an extension, to us): "I am giving you these words because they are *the* way of life. My intentions are good. If you will do these things, not only will your personal life be blessed, but society itself will be blessed."

Boundaries

To know God's blessings as individuals or as a society, God has established boundaries. Boundaries are the most freeing thing that can happen to anyone. That is why parents must realize the worst thing they could ever do to a child is never set a boundary.

A parent may say, "I am giving my child freedom."

No, you're not. Freedom is found within the consciousness of the real guidelines of life. When you set boundaries, you give the person an opportunity to express freedom.

Here is an easy illustration. If you are boating on the water, you find lanes to move from closed waterways to open waterways. Buoys are set as boundaries. Inside the buoys is where it's safe to traverse, but there's danger on the outside of them, such as rocks or shallow water that will damage or destroy the vessel.

The same is true of the white and yellow lines on the highway. Without them, drivers on the road are unable to tell if it is safe to pass a slower vehicle, or if they are even driving in the correct lane or direction.

The Decalogue is much the same. What's amazing about these ten words is how limited they are. God doesn't spell out every little detail. He sets the guidelines, the channel markers, the edge lines for your lane.

Here God gave His people guidelines from which they could discover life. I once heard someone aptly say that the God who gave the Israelites the Decalogue is the God who gave us Jesus. This is the God who loves us and is not trying to strike us down.

He is God who loves you so much that He was willing to bear your sins to bring you back into a right relationship with Him. The God of Mount Sinai is the God of Mount Calvary. If you separate God from His Decalogue, you are doing a grave injustice, not only to the Old Testament, but to all the revelations God gave for the coming of Jesus.

Covenant

Why do you keep the Decalogue? Is it because you know that the day you step out of line is the day God is going to send a thunderbolt from heaven and fry you on the spot? Or is it because you know God is coming to you, calling you to live in communion with Him? He wants to give you the guidelines so that you will grow and not only find the blessings of life, but the goodness of His grace showered upon you.

Consider this: a nation where no one lied, stole, coveted, or killed. What kind of nation would this be? It is almost impossible to imagine, but it is the one God wants for us. God said these words give us the way of life. God shows us life and death but asks us to choose life.

The Hebrew word most often translated into "commandments" is *mitsvah* (referring to instruction, as in Proverbs 2:1 and 3:1), where it speaks of storing God's words within us.[4] Another use of the word *mitsvah* in the Bible is to describe the terms of a contract (Jeremiah 32:11). *Mitsvah* can also refer to words of treaty and covenant. We see this in Exodus 24 when the people of Israel agreed as a community to follow all the words the Lord had spoken. Their agreement was a covenant between themselves and God, like America might make a treaty with Germany.

The use of the word *law* in translation for this word *mitsvah* is problematic, because it lends itself toward dead legalism and that isn't what this is about. Laws make us search for the narrowest restrictions: *"What can I get away with?"* Then we also judge others based on their adherence and interpretation of the law.

That is not what God was communicating here. He wasn't trying to keep an external authority imposed on us. God didn't create an ethical code. God sought to develop in people an attitude and an internal character that grows out of our gratefulness toward God.

I will make with them an everlasting covenant, that I will not turn away from doing good to them. And I will put the fear of me in their hearts, that they may not turn from me.
—Jeremiah 32:40

What is the new covenant Jeremiah talks about? Where are the commandments written in the new covenant? They are written on the heart not on tablets of stone (Jeremiah 31:31–33). So, when you go back and read the passage, you discover that God is creating the standards by which His people live, but these are simply standards—not externally imposed upon them. The commandments' intent is to become internalized so they can become the very expression of our lives. They are the ten words of God for us.

I am calling them *words* because the whole idea is that God's gift to the Israelites is not something to accomplish and it is not behavior modification. He is giving them something that will accomplish character formation.

Let me clarify it this way. The seventh commandment says, "You shall not commit adultery" (Exodus 20:14). I do not commit adultery, not because there's a law against it. If the only thing restraining me is fear of God's punishment, I don't have a good relationship with God or a good marriage. No, I don't commit adultery *because* I have a good relationship with God, and thus I honor my wife and our covenant relationship.

It isn't because I *must not* do it. It is because I *will not* do it. It is beautiful when we say, "I will not do that." Not because God says no, but because we want to experience God's purpose and intent for our lives.

You Know the Commandments

In the book of Mark, we read about a man who comes to Jesus and asks Him, "What must I do to inherit eternal life?" (Mark 10:17). What I want Jesus to say is, repent and be born again. But that is not what Jesus said to him. He said, "You know the commandments" (Mark 10:19).

If you take that statement out of the context of Scripture, it may seem like Jesus is saying something like: "Okay, you want to have eternal life? Start keeping the commandments."

But if Jesus said that, He would stand in contradiction to His own words from John 3:16. And Paul said in Ephesians 2:8 that we can't save ourselves: "For by grace you have been saved through faith. And this is not your own doing; it is the gift of God."

Jesus wasn't telling the man how to be saved. He was telling him how to live, because the way to eternal life is clearly revealed through the first of the commandments. If the man wanted to find salvation, he would first have to learn to love God with all his heart, soul, and mind (Matthew 22:37).

The ultimate purpose of the Decalogue isn't about being a rule follower. It's about learning to love God with the same depth of passion that He has for us.

WORKBOOK

Introduction Questions

Question: What comes to mind when you think of The Ten Commandments? What images or attributes of God do you think of in relation to His Decalogue? In what ways have these ten *words* made an impact on your life?

_____

_____

_____

_____

_____

_____

_____

_____

_____

_____

Question: Give an example of how a command or a standard can also be an expression of love. How does obeying God's words help us to understand His love for us and to show our love for Him?

_____

_____

_____

_____

_____

_____

_____

_____

_____

_____

_____

Question: Describe the time in your life when you entered into an intimate relationship with God. How did you become aware of your sin, and what prompted you to turn to Christ as your Savior? How has your life changed and what does it mean to have an ongoing walk with God?

_____

_____

_____

_____

_____

_____

_____

_____

_____

_____

_____

_____

Action: Research the impact of the Ten Commandments on society. What have famous theologians and political figures had to say about them? How has the Decalogue blessed those cultures that honored it?

Prayer: Our Father in heaven, by Your love You have created us in Your image. We give thanks for allowing us to know You in truth and confidence. We are amazed that as our great God, our Creator, You have revealed Yourself to us, Your creatures. You have revealed Your true nature through Your words of covenant love, and we are eternally grateful. We thank You for how You have shown us Your love and Your plans for us. Grant us the courage to obey You, for Your sake and ours. Amen.

Introduction Notes

_____

_____

_____

_____

_____

_____

_____

_____

_____

_____

_____

_____

_____

_____

_____

_____

_____

_____

CHAPTER ONE

The First Word:
No Other Gods

You shall have no other gods before me.
—Deuteronomy 5:7

After God's deliverance of the Israelites from their bondage in Egypt, He brought them to Mount Sinai. There God told them, "I have done all this for you and now I want to set before you the decision you have to make."

In the introduction, I referred to a passage in Exodus 19, which is God's introduction of Himself to Israel. It is also the first time God speaks to Israel as a whole about the covenant He made with their forefathers and was now making with them. In Deuteronomy 5, we find a parallel version of the commandments from Exodus 20:

And Moses summoned all Israel and said to them, "Hear, O Israel, the statutes and the rules that I speak in your hearing today, and you shall learn them and be careful to do them.

The LORD our God made a covenant with us in Horeb. Not with our fathers did the LORD make this covenant, but with us, who are all of us here alive today. The LORD spoke with you face to face at the mountain, out of the midst of the fire, while I stood between the LORD and you at that time, to declare to you the word of the LORD. For you were afraid because of the fire, and you did not go up into the mountain. He said:

"'I am the LORD your God, who brought you out of the land of Egypt, out of the house of slavery.

"'You shall have no other gods before me.'"

—Deuteronomy 5:1–7

Of all the words we have in the Bible, this is the only time God Himself spoke directly to the people of Israel. Everywhere else, God used a mediator to stand between Himself and those to whom He was speaking.

When God met with Israel and spoke to them at Mount Sinai, He gave them the opportunity to choose whether or not they would be His people. The covenant relationship was clearly established with the simple affirmation, "I am the LORD your God" (Deuteronomy 5:6).

Stop and think: God, the Eternal Creator, the Sovereign Lord, the Master of all that exists, takes the time to draw us into a personal relationship with Himself, making a place for us to meet directly with Him. These words were not only addressed to the people of Israel, but in a real sense, they are also addressed to us.

As I called attention to this in the introduction, the words of the Decalogue are an expression of God's love. Through them, God says, "Here is a pattern to follow and here are boundaries to remain within so that you can live a full and abundant life."

For example, if people in America would start today to obey all of God's words, our lives would not be adversely affected by the consequences of our selfish choices. There would be harmony in homes, in workplaces, in cities, and throughout our nation.

If that were to happen, I think we would be close to saying we had reached the kingdom of God on earth. When we live by these guidelines, we are in complete alignment and agreement with the God who created our world and who, therefore, understands how our lives work best together.

Significance to the Israelites

The first word that God speaks to the Israelites is: "I am the LORD your God.... You shall have no other gods before me" (Exodus 20:2–3).

This first word is the foundational concept upon which everything else is built. This is the first boundary. Before you continue on to the next word, you must understand that the entire Decalogue rests on this foundational fact, this *word*, "I am the LORD your God.... You shall have no other gods before me" (Deuteronomy 5:6–7). This is clearly a statement the nation of Israel would understand, and it is here where we as Christians rest our faith.

The people of Israel were surrounded by nations who worshiped other gods. Yet, God didn't take the time, nor go through the trouble, of making any further statement about these other gods. Some biblical scholars suggest that at this time in biblical history a true *monotheism* (the belief in the existence of only one God) didn't exist. Rather there was *henotheism*, a thinking that, yes, there may be other gods in the world, but you have one God.

I am inclined to agree with a Jewish scholar by the name of Yehezkel Kaufmann in his book, *The Religion of Israel,* when in essence he said, "Here is the actual birth of monotheism. Here is where it begins. I am God and you will not have any other. The language is not that of henotheism. It is a language of monotheism. It is important to recognize that Israel derives its faith from no other nation around it."[5]

At the time of the Exodus, no nation around Israel practiced monotheism. We cannot look to the cultures around them and say, "Israel got this from the Philistines and that from the Canaanites." Instead, God spoke directly to the nation: "I am Yahweh your God. You shall not have other gods beside Me." This point in history, when monotheism took root in the nation of Israel, marks a new beginning. It marks the beginning of the Judeo-Christian confidence in a single God.

Exclusive Relationship

The implications of the first words God spoke are numerous. The first thing that struck me is that God was obviously establishing an exclusive relationship with Israel: "I am your God. There is no other God except Me."

In other words, "I am claiming an exclusive relationship with you. I am expecting of you a singularity in your commitment to Me. No matter what other nations may do, or however they may pray, I am your God."

There is a Hebrew word, *tāmam,* which means "perfect."[6] God has commanded us to be perfect (Matthew 5:48). I am reminded of a beautiful excerpt regarding the ritual for the Lord's Supper, where it says, "Cleanse the thoughts of our hearts by the inspiration of thy Holy Spirit, that we may perfectly love thee and worthily magnify thy holy Name."[7] The word *tāmam* suggests that.

The idea of perfection is a Hebrew idea, not a Greek idea. In Greek philosophical thought, the idea of perfection had the sense of completion so there is nothing lacking. There is no want. There is nothing amiss.

If you take that definition, who of us would ever want to claim for a moment that we stand in any way perfect before God? We know ourselves all too well. I find a great deal of blessing in the old orthodox prayer that's often on my mind: "Lord Jesus Christ, Son of God, have mercy on me, a sinner"[8] (Luke 18:13).

We recognize how far short we fall, and we know we cannot possibly offer to God any sense of perfection. But, if we associate that word with the Hebrew concept of wholeness, it gives us a better understanding. Instead of using the word *perfect,* let's use the word *integrity.* God says, "I expect integrity in your relationship with Me. And that integrity is a sense of singularity and wholeness. The perfection I ask of you is not that you do everything perfectly well, but that your worship of Me and your relationship with Me is a whole relationship. It's a singular relationship."

Sometimes in the Old Testament, you discover that people are described as having two hearts. James states it in a different way. He says we have two minds, "For that person must not suppose that he will receive anything from the Lord; he is a double-minded man, unstable in all his ways" (James 1:7–8).

The only one who has a connection of integrity with God is the person who comes with all of his heart and all of his mind, understanding that the covenant he makes with God is a singular one.

An exclusive relationship with God is not so far-fetched when you compare it to marriage vows. When I conduct weddings, I ask the bride and groom to declare one to the other a singularity of commitment: "Forsaking all others, I pledge myself to you alone as long as we both shall live." That's integrity in relationship—wholeness. We understand that and we commit ourselves to faithfulness.

God calls Israel to this kind of exclusive relationship. You can't have Him *and* any other gods. He is your God. He wants an exclusive relationship with you.

Pragmatic Relationship

In my study of the first word, "have no other gods before me," I see in this that God was not only speaking of an exclusive relationship, but also a pragmatic relationship. It's not an intellectual exercise. Our relationship with God works in practical, everyday living.

God is telling Israel that a relationship with Him is not like the connections the pagan cultures around them have with their gods. These cultures had shrines and temples where they would bow down and worship their idols. God is not a theological idol that we can set up in an academic classroom or in our homes in some kind of prayer center and say, "This is where God is."

Jesus does not reside on a crucifix, however helpful that may be to us as we consider His sacrifice for our sins. He is not there. God breaks through into ordinary routines of life. This is a pragmatic covenant God is making with people. He is talking about a life-oriented relationship. He wants to be with us through the daily activities of our lives.

That would have great meaning to Israel. What God is saying to these people is that in the other religions around them, they worship their goddesses and gods so they can benefit from the fruit of their supposed powers. For example, the nations around them had goddesses and gods of fertility. If one wanted their fields to be fertile and productive, they would make a sacrifice based on that particular god's requirement so they could have an abundant harvest. The Lord God is saying to them, "I am your God; I am the source of your needs. You are to rely on Me for your security. You are to rely on Me for your social stability. I will provide all that, for I am indeed the Lord your God."

Think of security. In the book of Isaiah, when he said the people were foolish for running to Egypt for help to resist the enemy, he pointed out they were mere men (Isaiah 31:1–3). They were not God. The enemy only had horses and chariots, and these were not spiritual weapons. But Israel had God. Isaiah asked why they were not looking to God for help.

So, throughout the centuries, Israel was reminded and understood that it was God whom they could depend on.

It was God they could rely on for their security, their sub-sistence, and social stability. When we read how the prophets called Israel out for its failures, you will notice that socially the reason the nation was disintegrating was because they had failed to make God the center of their lives.

God was calling these people to a radically altered life-style. In Leviticus 18, when Israel was entering the Prom-ised Land, God's message to them was basically: "This is what I want you to understand. Your life is not to be like the Egyptians from which you came, and your life is not to be like the Canaanites where you are now going. I want you to live according to the pattern I set before you, be-cause I am the Lord. Ours is to be a pragmatic relationship that relates to everyday life."

A Defining Relationship

Ultimately, the ten words are more about God than they are about Israel. They are a moral photograph of who He is and what He expects. But these words only give a glimpse of His character. If you truly want to know who God is, read His word.

I think it's important to recognize that the Decalogue is a defining relationship. It's defining in that it reveals who God is. God wants you to know that He is God. It's also defining because you need to know who He wants you to be. It works in both directions.

I want you to make note of two principles. When God defines His relationship with us in this first word: He dis-tinguishes the difference between *the good* and *goods*.

You may ask what that means. Think what people's gods may be today: a god of money, a god of pleasure, a god of business, or a god of this or that.

All of these are not necessarily bad. Money isn't bad. It's the love of money that is the root of many evils (1 Timothy 6:10). Money is a good thing. But God says there is a difference between the *good* and *goods*. When you put goods first in your life and let them set your priorities, you are going to miss out on what God has for you and what He intended your life to be. But if you will put Him in first place, you'll discover that you also enjoy the goods that He, as the *good*, provided for you. And they will be a blessing to you.

The second thing to notice is that (except for some Catholic monastic orders) there is no Judeo-Christian tradition that suggests materiality is evil. In Greek philosophy, everything is god and the further away you get from god, the more materialistic you become. In materiality resides evil. You find that in Plato, too—evil is resident in materiality.

You won't find this philosophy in the Bible. Instead, you will see that material things are not bad. Goods are God-given and meant to be used a certain way. It is when we use those things outside of the boundaries God established that we run into a problem.

In this first word, God says, "I am giving you a defining relationship that not only defines who I am and defines how I want you to relate to Me, but also defines how your relationship should be to the world around you." This is what God was saying to the Israelites.

We can enjoy everything around us. God has created

all things. In the beginning, He said all of creation was good (Genesis 1). It is His good given to us. It is only when we mistake the order of our priorities that we violate this commandment, and we lose the blessings God has for us.

What does God say to us today? What is the significance of this word? The first word of God to us is also a fundamental reality. Putting the Ten Commandments on school walls is not going to do any good, unless people subscribe to those words. Our knowing all of the commandments will not make a difference until we accept the foundational statement that God is God, and that these words are not meant to box us into a pen, but to free us to experience the goodness of His creation based on the standards by which He created them.

Sovereign Creator

In her book, *Smoke on the Mountain,* which is about the Ten Commandments, Joy Davidman makes this observation about what the first commandment says, not only to the Israelites, but to us: "the voice is the same, and the word is the same. The universe is one process, created by one Maker."[9] She went on to observe that this belief in one God "is the fundamental assumption of modern science as well as that of timeless religion."[10]

Science is based on the assumption that we live in a universe. The law of gravity is not any different in Africa than it is in America. The speed of light is a constant, not different rates as though we are in a multiverse. We are in a universe. All of these laws are working together.

The Bible says the reason why all these work together is because all creation has its source in one God. There aren't a bunch of gods creating them and trying to conform them to their own whims. If that were so, then we would have a hodgepodge of creation instead of an orderly universe.

Imagine, for example, a number of engineers in a room. Let's suppose they are going to work on a project individually; everyone doing their own thing—whatever the project may be, such as designing a bridge. You have to wonder what's going to come out if everybody is working separately and creating their own thing.

When there's a master plan by a master creator, however, there is no doubt that the bridge will be one that functions safely and efficiently. The same is true of the laws of nature, which is why science and faith can and do coexist in harmony.

A number of years ago when I was teaching on Christian Beliefs, I ran across an article in which the author addressed why it is that scientific technology developed in the western world and not in the eastern world. He concluded that the Judeo-Christian tradition set the atmosphere in which science could be productively pursued.[11]

I know that we are supposed to be the children of enlightenment. In school we were taught that the Middle Ages were dark ages when nothing advanced. The only problem with that belief is if you read the scholarly writings of people who lived in those ages, they outstrip the people who live today. And more than that, the idea of the university was not born in the enlightenment. It was born in the old monasteries of the Christian faith and developed in Christian circles. I hope you are aware of the fact that universities in the United States of America were founded by Christians and almost every school was originally church related. It wasn't a bunch of atheists who said we needed religious educational institutions. These founders were people who believed in the God of the first commandment.

Rub of Exclusivism

This idea of exclusive relationships creates a rub in our day. Our primary word today is *tolerance*. We are supposed to be tolerant of everything. In fact, we are getting so broad minded, we say that nothing but space exists out there now. And we wonder: Where do we draw any lines and limits?

Tolerance says no one may be right, so therefore, everybody may be right. What we have in our own country is democracy running berserk. It has almost destroyed the educational system in this country. And it has pretty much destroyed the morals of this country. And so, we hear it said today, "That is your truth, but my truth is something else."

There can't be two truths if they are in conflict. Then the next step is to say there are no truths at all, and that's where we live today.

So, when there is a God who stands up and says, "I am God, and here are My words," we find a great deal of resistance. Part of that resistance is simply the fact that opposition today is not about principles and the Ten Commandments. It's about the fact that God has revealed

Himself to us. Because if God has revealed Himself, then we have an absolute truth. We don't vote on that in our schools. We don't vote on that in our society. God has said it. He is God, He has declared it and so it is the truth, and it doesn't make any difference what anybody else says.

But that is not what people want to hear. Even in biblical circles, scholars have written that God didn't really reveal the Decalogue to the Israelites; that instead, they worked it out through a historical, evolutionary process until they came out with the end result. Their idea was that the Ten Commandments were the result of what men had accomplished.

But if God has said it—if this was a revelation from the Eternal One who created all things, and this God has declared Himself—then this is His truth. It isn't for us to vote on whether we want to believe this or not. This is His truth. This is God's word.

God says He is God. And if He is God who created all things, then His word is the supreme word, the *last* word, and the ultimate reality by which the origin, nature, and destiny of human life is governed, and that includes you and me.

And if He is not God, then we might as well shuffle out of our churches with no benediction, because we would have no reason to be in church. To say that some man or some group came up with some rules and regulations doesn't even make sense. When I look at the meaning and significance of life and I am asking the question of my destiny, when I am dealing with death in the lives of other people and my own family, then I realize that nobody's idea is adequate. But if God has spoken and if His words are true, then this is the God who gives meaning and significance as we relate our lives to His words.

Rub of Obedience

Another point that rubs people wrong is the idea of obedience to God. God wants us to submit ourselves to Him. I have noticed that in some marriage ceremonies now, they want to remove the word submit. Why? We are not talking about women being subject to their husbands in the sense of domination, but rather being in a love relationship in which each is submitted to the needs of the other. And God calls us to be in that same submission to Him.

Some people have walked away from a relationship with Jesus Christ because such a life means submitting their lives to Him. The only true gospel is one of submission to Jesus Christ our Lord and Savior, to the Creator Father who has made us in His image, and who destined us for that which we cannot even begin to imagine—the glory that is to be ours in eternity.

There may be people who look at the Ten Commandments as God breathing fire down on Israel, because He was trying to control their lives and that the entire thread of His rules is to bring punishment on the rule breakers. But that is not true. What you find within the Decalogue is the love of God being presented to us.

The opposite of love in the Bible is not hate. It is wrath. That means, when God offers His words to us in love and we choose not to obey them, we are declaring that we are His enemies. That is when we experience His wrath—and

His wrath is as real as His love. The punishment for our sins is the consequence we bring upon ourselves when we live in opposition to God's love.

We are living in a world that is fragmented, and lives are being ripped apart because of it. We wonder why students are shooting each other in schools and workers are sabotaging their colleagues, and governments are oppressing their people. It is because we have stepped out of this fundamental fact that the Lord is our God. And if we place Him where He deserves as the head of all things, then we will know and experience His love in the fullness of its measure.

If we choose to place our other gods in the spot that is reserved for Him, we will know and experience the full measure of the consequences that comes when we live in opposition to Him.

If we will live in the guidelines of His obedience, we will know His love. But He is God; and not to know His love is to know His wrath.

In the book by C. S. Lewis, *The Lion, the Witch and the Wardrobe*, Mr. Beaver told Lucy that Aslan is a lion.

"Then he isn't safe?" said Lucy.

"Safe?" said Mr. Beaver, "don't you hear what Mrs. Beaver tells you? Who said anything about safe? 'Course he isn't safe. But he's good. He's the King, I tell you."[12]

Is God safe? He is God, and He is good. He loves us. He is Almighty God.

WORKBOOK

Chapter One Questions

Question: What are some reasons that people struggle with the exclusivity of Yahweh God? How did Jesus echo this exclusivity and why are so many unbelievers offended because of it? Why is monotheism still an important and relevant theological truth in our world today?

_____

_____

_____

_____

_____

_____

_____

_____

_____

Question: In what ways is God your Source, the One you rely on for every aspect of life and faith? What happens when you begin to look to other people, possessions, or ideas to give meaning, provision, and security to your life?

_____

_____

_____

_____

_____

_____

_____

_____

_____

_____

_____

Question: How does your relationship with God define every other relationship in your life? Describe a time when you began to pursue the _goods_ versus the _good_. How do you miss out on God's earthly blessings when the goods in your life take God's place in your heart?

_____

_____

_____

_____

_____

_____

_____

_____

_____

_____

Action: Find recent examples in culture, education, psychology, politics, religion, and even church, of how "tolerance" and the idea of different or personal truths created confusion and chaos. How would each of these situations be changed by a return to absolute truth? In what ways do you observe rebellion against God causing this rejection of His truth? How can believers live and interact with integrity in a society bereft of truth while continuing to "speak the truth in love" (Ephesians 4:15)?

Prayer: Lord God, we bow before You because You are the Lord Almighty. You are the one true God. Although the world around us discards our faith and even scoffs at its significance, we find that through the years of history and up to our present day, people have discovered when they walk within the boundaries You have set, there are blessings aplenty. But when we step out of those boundaries, Your wrath becomes the experience of our fallenness. Guide us, we pray, as we think on these things. In Christ's name we pray. Amen.

Chapter One Notes

CHAPTER TWO

The Second Word: Worship Yahweh

You shall not make for yourself a carved image, or any likeness of anything that is in heaven above, or that is on the earth beneath, or that is in the water under the earth. You shall not bow down to them or serve them; for I the LORD your God am a jealous God, visiting the iniquity of the fathers on the children to the third and fourth generation of those who hate me, but showing steadfast love to thousands of those who love me and keep my commandments.
—Deuteronomy 5:8–10

Only take care, and keep your soul diligently, lest you forget the things that your eyes have seen, and lest they depart from your heart all the days of your life. Make them known to your children and your children's children—how on the day that you stood before the LORD your God at Horeb, the LORD said to me, "Gather the people to me, that I may let them hear my words, so that they may learn to fear me all the days that they live on the earth, and that they may teach their children so." And you came near and stood at the foot of the mountain, while the mountain burned with fire to the heart of heaven, wrapped in darkness, cloud, and gloom.

Then the LORD spoke to you out of the midst of the fire. You heard the sound of words, but saw no form; there was only a voice. And he declared to you his covenant, which he commanded you to perform, that is, the Ten Commandments, and he wrote them on two tablets of stone. And the LORD commanded me at that time to teach you statutes and rules, that you might do them in the land that you are going over to possess.

Therefore watch yourselves very carefully. Since you saw no form on the day that the LORD spoke to you at Horeb out of the midst of the fire, beware lest you act corruptly by making a carved image for yourselves, in the form of any figure, the likeness of male or female, the likeness of any animal that is on the earth, the likeness of any winged bird that flies in the air, the likeness of anything that creeps on the ground, the likeness of any fish that is in the water under the earth. And beware lest you raise your eyes to heaven, and when you see the sun and the moon and the stars, all the host of heaven, you be drawn away and bow down to them and serve them, things that the LORD your God has allotted to all the peoples under the whole heaven. But the LORD has taken you and brought you out of the iron furnace, out of Egypt, to be a people of his own inheritance, as you are this day.

—Deuteronomy 4:9–20

It may come as a surprise to some of us that the Ten Commandments so called—the ten words God gave to the Israelites—are not represented the same way in all confessional groups of Christianity. Some people regard what we are calling the second word as part of the first word.

Martin Luther emphasized that the first commandment was that we should worship the Lord our God *and* not make any graven idols. The second commandment, in his view, was brought right over into the first commandment. Other scholars have done that also.[13]

I, however, differ with Luther. I see two different ideas presented here. In the first word, God declares an exclusive relationship with Israel: "There is no other God besides Me, and you are not to have any other god but Me. I claim exclusive allegiance from you." This was after God had spoken to the people and given them the opportunity of deciding whether they would follow Him or not. They had answered, "Yes, we will follow you" (Exodus 19:8, paraphrased).

Upon their agreement, God said, "Here are the words by which I want you to understand how our relationship is going to exist. This is the covenant I'm establishing with you. And the first is that you shall be committed to Me exclusively."

When we looked at the first word, we noted that it was an exclusive relationship, but it was also a pragmatic relationship, and a defining relationship. We saw how that first commandment was important as a base for everything Israel was going to develop within the nation. The second, third, and fourth words build on the first word. The second word deals with the question of worship. In this commandment, God said, "You will worship Me in one way, not with idols and not with images."

In Deuteronomy, Moses is careful to say that these images become corrupting factors when you allow them to usurp a place in your worship. It seems to me that one of the reasons why this should be a second commandment—and not swallowed up into the first—is because worship is such an essential part of our relationship with God.

Worship: The Overlooked Element

I remember hearing a seminary professor say worship is the most important thing we do, because according to the book of Revelation, everything that is part of our earthly life right now is going to pass away—except worship. Worship will be an eternal relationship between God and His children. Since worship (which goes beyond singing songs on Sunday) is so important for us, it's interesting to me that it is often ignored.

In all my biblical studies for my divinity degree, my master's degree, and my doctoral program, apparently worship was not deemed important enough to spend a class looking at its historical perspective so that we could fully understand what worship truly is.

I had no course on worship in the Old Testament. While studying and preparing to teach about the Decalogue, I realized I knew about the sacrifices and the Psalms, yet as far as worship itself, I did not have a concrete idea of how all of it came together. Worship matters and is vital to our covenant with God.

We often feel that going to church doesn't make a difference one way or another. According to the Word of God, it makes a big difference. In a similar fashion as Israel being called together before the Lord, church draws us together so that we might worship Him.

Some people say, "Well, I can worship God outside in nature." I won't argue with that. I've done that. I have been keenly aware of God in my life outside of the church building; and I admit that in the beauty of nature, you have something unrivaled by the most magnificent cathedral that has ever been built. But one thing is lacking. Out there, I'm by myself. Out there, the community of believers is not together, encouraging one another and devoting ourselves to the attention we should be giving to God as our Heavenly Father. Coming to church is not an idle thing we do on Sundays. As the people of God worship together, we become a united and dynamic influence that is enabled to make a difference in our world. When we fail to worship together as a church, we fail to recognize the unity of the body of Christ, for which Jesus prayed. In John 17:20–26, we read His prayer:

I do not ask for these only, but also for those who will believe in me through their word, that they may all be one, just as you, Father, are in me, and I in you, that they also may be in us, so that the world may believe that you have sent me. The glory that you have given me I have given to them, that they may be one even as we are one, I in them and you in me, that they may become perfectly one, so that the world may know that you sent me and loved them even as you loved me. Father, I desire that they also, whom you have given me, may be with me where I am, to see my glory that you have given me because you loved me before the foundation of the world. O righteous Father, even though the world does not know you, I know you, and these know that you have sent me. I made known to them your name, and I will continue to make it known, that the love with which you have loved me may be in them, and I in them.

I look at this second commandment as an important one, because it talks to the Israelites about their worship and about what should *not* be a part of their worship. Look at God's prohibitions and bring it into our present time with questions about how we would understand His instructions if they were given to us today. It's quite different in some ways than the Israelites would have viewed it over three thousand years ago.

I AM God

When we look at what God is saying to the Israelites, it is very clear who He is. In fact, you don't need much explanation, because He says, I am Yahweh. That is the covenant name God gave to Moses: I am Yahweh your God.

Studies done on the name of Yahweh could fill half of our libraries, and we still would only have uncovered the tip of its full meaning. Some scholars suggest Yahweh means "I AM," which is how we have seen it in our translation of Scripture. God said to Moses: "Say this to the people of Israel: 'I AM has sent me to you'" (Exodus 3:14b). We associate that with what Jesus said: "I am the bread of life" (John 6:35). "I am the light of the world" (John 8:12). "I am the good shepherd" (John 10:11). And the most startling of all: "...before Abraham was, I am" (John 8:58).

Do you want to know why the religious leaders of the day picked up stones to stone Jesus? Because they understood He was claiming to be God and they rejected His claim as blasphemy.

William. F. Albright, in his book *From the Stone Age to Christianity*, said there is another way *Yahweh* could be translated. He wrote that the name of God should be interpreted, "I cause to be what is."[14]

Why does God forbid the Israelites to have images? Because if you make God in the image of the sun, moon, mountain, river, or tree, you are taking a part of creation and identifying God with some part of it. God, according to Scripture, cannot be identified with anything in creation. He stands outside of it. He stands above it. These ancient peoples looked at the sun, moon, stars, and the river because of the powers associated with them. When you associate God with these powers, you are not representing Him at all. I AM is the One who has created them and as such, He is beyond all of creation.

God is everything that we are, yet infinitely more. Some may ask: Why do you believe God is a Person? It's because we are persons created in His image; and if He has created us as persons, He cannot be less than we are; He has to be more than we are. That's what God was saying to the Israelites. He is more than anything we take as an image, so we don't lower God to that level.

Idols Delimit God

As God spoke to the Israelites, He prohibited idols and images because they delimited Him. Idols delimit God in terms of His *nature*. In other words, images and sculptures could only attempt to define a portion of His nature, and thus would limit the people's ability to recognize that God was far more than the object they were worshiping.

Images limit God in the idea of His *presence*. When a Canaanite went into his temple and declared that Baal is the god of his country, he was saying that his god was circumscribed (limited) to that particular place, not somewhere else, not omnipresent.

This is why God didn't want to be made in the form of an image. Because He knew if we created an image of Him, we would begin to think of Him as no different than all the other gods and our relationship with Him would be stunted as a result.

I have often said that the title, "the house of God," is an unfortunate one in the sense that we think of the church as being the place where God lives. If I were God, the one place I would *not* want to live is in church. Not much goes on in church except on Sunday mornings and maybe Wednesday nights. Life happens outside of the church— in the business world, in recreational places of our country, in our families and in our homes. That's where life is going on, and if God isn't in those places, then He is irrelevant.

Images also limit God in terms of the *power* He exercises. God wants to do so much more than throw down lightning bolts or raise up crops. To see God as the power of the sun may suggest His great power, but it limits God. If you see God as the power of the storm—just as the Canaanites considered Baal as their storm-god—you delimit God so that His nature is no different than the god of the Canaanites. When the storms roared, thunder cracked, and lightening flashed, people would say, "Here is our god at work."

God's presence, His power, His very nature, is limited when represented by idols. When we come to worship, He doesn't want us to make an image of Him, because the minute we do that, we begin to corrupt the idea of who He is and what He is about.

A Distinctive Break

I think one distinct reason God had for not wanting any images made to represent Him is because God wanted His people to have a distinctive break between what they had been in the past and who they had become.

Nations all around Israel had idols and images. It was true in Egypt. It was true in the desert. And it was true of the land they were entering.

God spoke to His people and said there needed to be a discontinuity in what they had been (slaves) and what they had now become (free). He wanted them to be a different people. This is exactly what he said in terms of their conduct in the previous commandment. He didn't want them to live like the Egyptians or the Canaanites. God wanted them (and us) to live in accordance with who He is and how He directed them. Righteousness is that which is in accordance with His nature and what separates His people from the people around them.

You can see a parallel to this today when Christians are being mocked for saying they've been born again. The term means not only a new beginning, but also a difference in our lives. As you read through the New Testament, one thing is clear—God calls us to be a different people. If we don't labor to make a distinction between ourselves and the unbelieving world, then what right do we have to claim we have a message any different than what the world has?

We are called to be a different people. That's why some people don't want to be Christians. That's why some people come to the point of knowing what Jesus Christ says about who He is, and then turn and walk away from Him.

God said to the Israelites, "I'm not worried about your acceptance among the Canaanites and all the other *'ites* that are running around. I want you to be My people, and this is the way I want you to worship Me. Not with images."

It was very important in a practical sense. They were distinguishing themselves—who they were and what God wanted them to be.

Trust an Unseen God

God desired that they trust in Him alone, without any visual images. Stop and think: *"That was radical, not only to suggest it to people, but to **expect** it of them."*

One of the hardest things about being a Christian is worshiping a God who is "unseen." It would be so much easier if there were a visual image we could lay hold upon. We want that in our lives. We base our decisions on what we can see and feel. In this day of management skills, we set goals. We create visual markers, so we know when we have reached what we're working toward. How can you measure something unless it's in the form of a visual idea? You must have something for comparison.

Here were these Israelites with all the people around them and all their images and idols and God said, "Okay, you're My people. No images. No idols. No visual aids. I want you to follow Me. I want you to rest your confidence in Me." It meant they were going to live by the experience they had of God's work in their lives. Don't you wonder why repeatedly in the Old Testament, and even the New Testament, the story of Egypt is told? Why did the Israelites always talk about Egypt? For the same reason Christians always talk about their conversion experience.

I can point to an exact spot in my life where I drove down a stake. I can say, "God met me as a seventeen-year-old high-school student one Sunday night. Here is where He cornered me as I sat in a church pew, and He called me to be a proclaimer of the gospel of Jesus Christ."

It's been a revolutionary moment in my life to this present day. It's an anchor, because there have been those times when my soul gave way and I wondered how I could keep this up. Sometimes, I've wondered if I'm going to get to the end and discover that all I have been preaching isn't true. How do I know I'm walking in the right direction? Invariably I come back to that moment as a seventeen-year-old boy when I knew God spoke to me and He changed the course of my life.

You could give testimony to something similar. You may have had an experience, a turning point in your life—a place where God has said to you, "I don't want you to have idols; I want you to lean on Me in faith." That meant leaning on an experience based on faith.

Why did Jesus say, "It's better for you if I go away so I can send the Holy Spirit?" (John 16:7, paraphrased). It's better because the Holy Spirit can be in every person's life; and His presence—which is so vital to a continuing relationship—is necessary and good for us.

God Speaks

Here is the revolutionary part. God promised Israel that He was not going to communicate to His people through idols and images. He was going to communicate with words. He spoke to them. Here at the mountain, directly. Later on, through prophets.

Through my studies I've discovered that the revelation of God's Word is continually under attack, and it's a contention among many scholars to this day.

Regarding the Ten Commandments, they say the people came together and borrowed various ideas from groups of people in the area. The idea that God *spoke* a word to them is unacceptable.

The great battle going on in biblical studies is whether God has revealed Himself, not simply in some kind of experience, but through propositional truth—God communicating to His people so they can understand Him. The reason for debate is because if God has spoken, then that word is *absolute*. People, however, don't want absolute truth, because they think it means they cannot make their own decisions. That shakes people up.

When God spoke to Israel, He reminded them that they had His word and the experience of His deliverance of bringing them out of Egypt. His words were remembered when New Testament writers kept pointing back to the prophets: this is according to what Isaiah said; this is according to Jeremiah. Thus, we experience revelation when we study Scripture and come away from a passage saying, "God has spoken a word to me." That word is vital in our relationship with God.

Idols and images are not needed, because God offers us a practical and personal experience. We can connect that word received from God with our own experiences in life, for God has told us who He is and who He wants us to be.

Images: Past and Present

The only way we can conceptualize any truth is with a mental image. What do you think when you hear the word *God*? What is the image in your mind?

The picture you create can show your perception of God, and it can be a wrong one. Some people hear *God* and think of a great bearded tyrant sitting up on a cloud with all this power, waiting for an excuse to smite anybody. Some picture a man in a suit who's ready to cut a deal with anyone who pays the right price or earns enough points doing good deeds.

J. B. Phillips wrote a book titled, *Your God Is Too Small*. In that book, he established that many people's mental image of God is less than who God really is.[15]

We have what are called *anthropomorphisms* in the Bible. We read references to the *hand of God*, the *eye of God,* and the *ear of God.* So, we form a human image in our mind. But "God is spirit" (John 4:24) with none of our physical features. So, although God says we are not to make any images of Him, you and I still come up with a mental image of who we believe God is, based on our life experiences and what we read about Him in Scripture or in books based on other people's interpretation of who

God is.

You may wonder what's wrong with that. Nothing, from the standpoint that visualization is vital to our understanding of the universe we live in. We are physical beings, and therefore, we best understand things when they are given a physical form. The problem comes when we begin to box God in according to our images—that God feels how we think He feels or acts the way we think He acts.

When we try to put into God those ideas that are our own, we can subtly make an image that's nothing like the real God. In fact, many people have an issue with God because of the image they created of Him during their growing-up years. They don't want to have anything to do with God, because they have an incorrect image of God.

We know that even as Moses was on Mt. Sinai receiving the commandments, the people were below making a golden calf (Exodus 32), a visual image to worship. Later when the kingdom of Israel was divided, Jeroboam of the northern kingdom set up golden calves at Dan and Bethel (1 Kings 12:25–33). When Ezekiel saw a vision, it was God showing him idolatry in the temple (Ezekiel 8:7–13).

But the idolatry in the New Testament took on a different form. This time it was the Law (or rather the Jewish religious leaders' interpretation of the Law) that became their idol. Because Jesus didn't live up to their interpretation of who the Messiah would be and what the Messiah would do, they refused to accept that Jesus was in fact the Son of God, Immanuel, God with us (Matthew 1:23; John 5:18).

This leads us to our current condition. And I start by

looking at you and me. The science that has developed in the Western world—as well as the thoughts of philosophy that directly impact how we interact with the world around us—were not part of people's lives during biblical times. They were nomads who created gods out of objects that represented what they pictured their gods would look like. Like the Pharisees and Sadducees, Christians today do not craft physical idols to set up in shrines and temples. But we do create images that direct how we worship.

When we come to worship, we must worship Him as He is, not according to *our* image of Him. It is true we don't have golden calves in Christian worship, but we have other gods, which people talk about all the time. The god of success. The god of wealth. The god of happiness. People bow down to their bank account and the social rung of the ladder. Those are obvious ones we can see.

Religious Idols

I want to press this further. The gods of today are subtle. They are also cultic images. Some people direct their worship to a crucifix. Their image of God is controlled by the image of Christ on the cross. Is Christ on the cross a wrong thing? No. It isn't a problem unless it becomes the controlling image or idol we worship.

It isn't the love of Jesus that breaks up churches, but our traditions and religious idols. Pastors and church leaders bow to the idol of a successful ministry. People concentrate on numbers rather than spiritual growth. Counting noses is an idol to us in ministry. Church growth has too often become achieving spiritual ends by secular means.

Leaders who fall spiritually rarely start out to become what they became. They certainly never intended to end up where they ended, broken and with all their mistakes exposed for the entire world to see. When you want success and it becomes an idol, the grief and pain are terrible to watch.

Neal Gabler, a famed movie critic and Hollywood historian, wrote a book titled, *Life: The Movie*. The subtitle is *How Entertainment Conquered Reality*. His thesis affirmed that all forms of commercialism today must have an entertainment value. Basically, every American institution, from education to religion, is transforming because of entertainment. The megachurch attracts clients (rather than worshipers) by devising an entertaining worship service through rock music, light shows, cappuccino carts, and the like. They're trying to make people feel like they are at a rock concert, and religion is thrown in as extra.[16]

That last part of his analysis really gripped me: religion is thrown in as an extra.

My intention is not to pass judgment on any particular group or church. What I am saying is that idols do exist. And they can exist in any kind of church. They can be religious idols or cultic idols, or they can simply be materialistic idols of our culture. Many people who sit in churches are those who, unfortunately, still have their idols with them and they don't know or understand that God says, no idols.

Doctrinal Idols

The last form of idolatry I want to address is theological and doctrinal idols. Even we, who name the name of Christ, can be so brutal to each other because we identify with our theological/doctrinal group rather than identify ourselves as Christians. This is not saying that doctrines are wrong or unimportant. What it *is* saying is that sometimes we have lost Christ where we have made ideas or traditions into idols.

Consider our interpretation of communion: whether we use wine or grape juice; if it actually becomes His blood or is only a symbol of it; or if we have to be a member of a specific church in order to take part in the sacrament. Communion can become an idol if we're more focused on being *right* than we are in being *obedient* to what God has ordained.

The great debates about the inerrancy of Scripture have torn people apart over the years, myself included. Squabbles about how to run a church program or whether or not we should boycott a specific business, book, or film have all too often come at the cost of the unity of the body of Christ. When the Lord's people are so focused on their *interpretations* of who God is and what He has called us to do, we become divisive and dismissive. We fail to exhibit the love of Jesus Christ.

God calls His people to worship Him without any idols in our hearts. I know the difficulties. I know the struggles. I know the battles. My heart is involved in what I have said, because I feel deeply about these issues, and yet at the same time I know the wrong perspective can usurp the place of God in our lives. God said to the Israelites, "If you allow idols to come into your lives and take over your worship, it will distort My people 'to the third and fourth generation'" (Deuteronomy 5:9).

In other words, idolatry affects the lives of everyone around us, including our children, grandchildren, and great-grandchildren.

Let's keep our faith clear, so that we—and they—know it is God whom we worship.

WORKBOOK

Chapter Two Questions

Question: How would you define *worship*? What activities or attitudes constitute worship? How are you experiencing both personal and corporate worship in your life and why is each important?

_____

_____

_____

_____

_____

_____

_____

_____

_____

_____

Question: How are you as a Christian different and distinct from the world around you? Are there ways in which you have adopted the worship mentality of the world, or of your life before Christ, instead of worshiping the true God in the way that He prescribes?

_____

_____

_____

_____

_____

_____

_____

_____

_____

_____

Question: What are some subtle idols that you have seen in the lives of believers, including religious or doctrinal idols that are exalted over obedience to God and a relationship with Him? How have idols destroyed churches? What idols do you personally have to guard against?

_____

_____

_____

Action: Have you ever put "limits" on God? For example, do you think of Him as only in some places but not others, or do you focus on certain attributes of His but ignore others (i.e. only loving but not just, or only righteous but not kind)? God's Word will give you a correct understanding of Him, replacing any faulty images that you have created. Begin a study of biblical theology to learn God's attributes. Contact your pastor to recommend a good study book you can understand. Ask God to reveal a complete and correct "image" of Himself to you through His Word.

Prayer: Our Father, it seems like it would be simpler to deal with golden calves, idols of wood and stone that we can see. While in other countries people have physical idols, we are grateful that You have delivered us from the bondage that demands such from worshipers. We don't bow before such idols, but we have set up our own idols that destroy the unity of Christ. Whether it's arguments about traditions or ideas that are less consequential, we have allowed these to take priority. May we not take our personal preferences and make them into idols before which everyone else must bow. Help us, Father, to follow You in faith to the best of our ability and understanding. We need the leadership of Your Holy Spirit. In Christ's name, we pray. Amen.

Chapter Two Notes

CHAPTER THREE

The Third Word: Don't Profane My Name

You shall not take the name of the LORD your God in vain, for the LORD will not hold him guiltless who takes his name in vain.

—Exodus 20:7

The third word is a brief word, but a very important one from the seventh verse of Exodus 20. When you go back to study history and other cultures, it's interesting to think about the significance of a name. In many cultures, names have a great deal of meaning. Not so much in our own culture. I feel names have lost their value in Western Civilization. We tend to choose names because we like the sound of them. Granted, maybe there is someone in the family who has that name, so it's passed on to the new generation, but beyond that, there isn't much significance tied to them.

I am convinced that as far as the government is

concerned, my identity is a number. Forget your name, but don't forget your number. It almost makes you think about the book of Revelation.

In the Old Testament you can note how often names have specific meaning that is of great importance. Children were given names that said something about their birth or specifics about them, like a future purpose or dreams of the parents. Noah's grandfather's name, Methuselah, means, "When he is dead, it shall be sent."[17] *It* being the great flood that covered the world in God's judgment of mankind's complete rejection of Him.

God also gave certain people their names. He changed Abram's name to Abraham to signify that many nations would come from him (Genesis 17:5–8). God gave Isaac, one of the patriarchs, a name that means "laughter" (Genesis 17:19). Sarai (given the name Sarah, Genesis 17:15) laughed when she heard about having a child in her old age (Genesis 18:12).

Jacob—not a particularly admirable person, though one of the patriarchs—had a name that meant deceiver, an accurate description of him because he cheated his brother out of his birthright and blessing (Genesis 25:29–34; Genesis 27). Even when he met God at Bethel, he tried to work a deal telling God he would follow Him if He would do something for him (Genesis 28:18–32). Jacob sought the Lord when life became difficult for him. But God took this man, renamed him Israel, and declared that through his line, God would reveal His name and salvation to the world (Genesis 32:28).

Names have power. In some cultures, it is believed that knowing a person's true name gives one power over another. So, a false name is given in order to protect oneself from curses and dark powers. That practice is not totally absent from the Bible. There is a sense of having control by knowing one's name. In Genesis 1, God said He was going to create Adam and Eve in His own image, and man was going to have dominion over all the earth. In Genesis 2, we read that Adam is given the privilege of naming the animals. Now, to you or me that doesn't mean anything. In Hebrew culture, that would be significant, because giving a name to these animals expressed dominance—or the dominion of man—over animals. So, what seems to us to be a nice little story is in actuality an expression of the image of God at work in Adam.

What's in a Name?

What does a name really mean? I think sometimes it has a great deal more significance than I have suggested to you. Shakespeare wrote in *Othello*, "Who steals my purse steals my trash; 'tis something, 'tis nothing.... But he that filches from me my good name robs me of that which not enriches him, and makes me poor indeed."[18]

I remember my mother impressing upon me at an early age that my name was important. How I conducted myself and how I lived before others was, not only a reflection of me and my name, but of my family. I bore the name of Coker and so everything I did reflected on the family. As a child growing up, I thought my name was important.

I've run into many situations where the importance of my name has been obvious. When I signed a mortgage, they wanted my name. The printed name on paper was worthless until I signed it. By signing, I accepted responsibility for the debt and gave my oath to repay it.

Consider the Declaration of Independence. For all of its eloquence, conviction, and passion, it's merely a document. The true power (and value) of the Declaration of Independence comes from the names of the men who signed the document, knowing that in doing so, they and their loved ones could be tried and executed for treason against the King of England if their cause failed.

Profanity: What Does It Mean?

It's easy to look at the first two words, which stated to have no other gods before God and not to make an image of Him, and clearly understand what they meant. But this third word—"You shall not take my name (lift up my name) unto emptiness or meaninglessness"—what does it mean?

It meant that as a kid, I didn't use God's name as a curse word. Profanity was saying, "God damn you," when I got mad at someone. But that is not taking God's name in vain. Those are not empty words without meaning. They're a curse, calling on God to strike someone down and send them straight to hell.

That's not a nothing statement; it is a *wrong* statement that should not be used. What it conveys is that a person is passing judgment that they have no right to pass. Only God holds an eternal soul in His hand to make that kind of judgment. While we should never relegate God's name to a curse or use it profanely, God was speaking about something far deeper when He warned Israel of the danger that came from using His name in vain.

The literal Hebrew translation for the third word that God speaks here is, "You shall not lift up the name of your God for the falseness."[19]

Merriam-Webster defines *vain* as useless, idle, worthless, foolish, and irreverent.[20]

When God talks about the idea of not profaning His name, He is telling them that it is dangerous to take that which is holy and use it as though it were common or worthless. When we devalue God's name, we devalue His power and authority in our lives. When that happens, we begin to allow other things to take His place, which leads us back to idolatry and the worship of other gods.

Consider the words spoken to Ezekiel, who was a prophet of God when the Israelites had been taken into captivity in Babylon. Ezekiel told them God revealed to him why Jerusalem had been destroyed. He spoke to them this word about profaning God's name.

The word of the LORD came to me: "Son of man, when the house of Israel lived in their own land, they defiled it by their ways and their deeds. Their ways before me were like the uncleanness of a woman in her menstrual impurity. So I poured out my wrath upon them for the blood that they had shed in the land, for the idols with which they had defiled it. I scattered them among the nations, and they were dispersed through the countries. In accordance with their ways and their deeds I judged them. But when they came to the nations, wherever they came, they profaned my holy name, in that people said of them, 'These are the people of the LORD, and yet they had to go out of his land.' But I had concern for my holy name, which the house of Israel had profaned among the nations to which they came.

"Therefore say to the house of Israel, Thus says the Lord GOD: It is not for your sake, O house of Israel, that I am about to act, but for the sake of my holy name, which you have profaned among the nations to which you came. And I will vindicate the holiness of my great name, which has been profaned among the nations, and which you have profaned among them. And the nations will know that I am the LORD, declares the Lord GOD, when through you I vindicate my holiness before their eyes. I will take you from the nations and gather you from all the countries and bring you into your own land. I will sprinkle clean water on you, and you shall be clean from all your uncleannesses, and from all your idols I will cleanse you. And I will give you a new heart, and a new spirit I will put within you. And I will remove the heart of stone from your flesh and give you a heart of flesh. And I will put my Spirit within you, and cause you to walk in my statutes and be careful to obey my rules."

—Ezekiel 36:16–27

The reason this passage is so important is because God had invited Israel into a relationship with Him, but they had profaned His holy name. The important thing is, how did they do this? Did they go around saying phrases we would use as curse words today? In this passage, God says they profaned His holy name in two different ways: by their conduct and by the condition of their hearts.

Profanity in Conduct

When we read Israel's history, we see a people who worshiped the Lord with their mouths and their sacrifices, but whose hearts were far from Him. This is important because when we think about this third commandment, we see that it's not only our voices that can be used to take God's name for nothing, it is our lives and conduct. If what we say and do fails to measure up to the profession of faith we make as people of God, we profane the name of God. We have taken His name in vain because we have transferred His name upon ourselves, yet our actions show a lack of reverence for the power of His name.

Years ago, a friend loaned his houseboat to my family for a week. The first night, as I was sitting on the front deck of the boat, a fellow from the next boat over walked up, stuck out his hand, and introduced himself. He said, "I hear you are a man of God."

His bluntness took me by surprise, but isn't that my profession? Isn't that exactly what I say about myself? Even as he said it, I thought, "Yes, that is what I represent."

My life needs to represent the profession I make. That is why when a preacher acts contradictory to the purpose of God, he is out of the will of God. He has taken on a profession and said to the world, "This is who I am." Failure to live up to that profession is a reproach toward God. We see that each time another news scandal breaks about a leader in one of our churches living completely contrarily to the message they proclaim.

That is not only true of preachers but lay people, too. You go to church on Sunday. People know you profess to be a believer in Jesus Christ. They know you represent yourself with the people of God. But you profane the name of God by your conduct when you live in a way that is the opposite of what you affirm on Sunday.

Profanity in Condition

Your life reflects something of who you are. The condition of your heart and life reflects upon God the same way your behavior as a child reflects on your family.

As a child of God, it is important to me that my life should measure up to the life God has called me into. In the times when I fail to do that, I discover that God never gives me any peace until I deal with that issue. I must make right that which separates me from what I know I ought to be. That's what it means when we say we are repentant; it means we recognize our actions have been out of alignment with God and we are taking action to come back into agreement with Him.

When God spoke to the Israelites at the base of the mountain, He didn't give them a rule having to do with the way they pronounced His name. However, as time passed, Jewish tradition became fixated on keeping the name of the Lord holy with their lips. By the time Jesus was born, the Pharisees wouldn't even pronounce the name of God. They believed that because God is holy and His name is righteous, that man—who is unrighteous—should not utter His name aloud.

Yet when Jesus confronted the Pharisees, He made it a point to show them the vanity of their actions when He said, "You hypocrites! You travel over land and sea to win a single convert, and when you have succeeded, you make them twice as much a child of hell as you are" (Matthew 23:15 NIV). Their conduct and condition did not reflect that they belonged to God.

What a word this is for us! I look at Ezekiel and read

about these people who profane the word of God. But then God declared that He is going to vindicate the holiness of His name, and that He is going to redeem the nation out of exile and bring them back into the land that is His land. He promised to sprinkle clean water on them and to make them clean. He declared that He is going to take their idols away and make them a new people.

God still makes us a new people. He is still forgiving. He is still a merciful God who cleanses us and transforms our lives, so our conduct and condition reflect His.

Representing God

When God said to Israel, "You will not *lift up* My name in vain" (see Exodus 20:7), the word He used did not mean "to speak." The Hebrew word used is *nāśā'*, which means "to lift up" or "to carry, to bear continuously."[21] It is not only what we *say* about the name of Yahweh; it's what we *do* and how we live. As we live before others and represent to our world the God whose name we call upon, our lives ought to reflect His pattern and example so that others can look at us and say, "Maybe I don't believe what that person believes, but that is a good person. That life represents Yahweh."

The pressing issue is: Do our lives represent God?

We glory in the fact Jesus Christ died for the sins of the world and He is our Savior and Lord. But do we live in such a way that we honor Him?

Look at Israel again. When God said not to lift up His name, it's possible to translate this as, "You shall not syncretize My name with idols," because the word translated as "vain" in Exodus 20:7 is the Hebrew word *shaw*, which indicates nothingness,[22] and that word can also be used of idols.

Isaiah said that an idol is nothing (Isaiah 44:9). Paul also wrote in 1 Corinthians 8:4, "An idol has no real existence."

What are idols? Idols are nothing. Some scholars think God is saying to the Israelites that they can't syncretize His name with the worship of these pagan people around them. Don't try to put these two people groups together. Don't try to unify or harmonize two opposites. This has even been done in our lifetime by some religious groups.

Don't look at what others have done. Take time to look at this passage in Exodus and ask if you've taken God's name in vain. And if so, how?

We could probably name a lot of ways. We talk about the Israelites syncretizing the worship of Yahweh with all these idols, but what about us today when we try to live so close to the world? What about when we allow the model and the pattern of our lives to be based on what's going on around us in the world rather than on the beauty of Jesus?

Why is it that our young people are finding their models, not in the elders, deacons, or pastors of the church, but often in people whose lives are so rotten and defiled that if we knew them personally we could never admire them? Why do we do that? Is it because while naming the name of Christ in our personal lives, we have also sought to live as close to the world as we can?

What about the model we choose for the church? Jesus did not say to lift up a technique of church growth so we can draw the world to Him. Jesus said, "And I, when I am lifted up from the earth, will draw all people to myself" (John 12:32).

The secret is not found in having this model or that model according to business practices, and I am not knocking business. Business has its proper practice. What I am saying is that the church is not a business. The church is a people belonging to God. If we exalt Him, if our lives model Him and people can see in us the pattern and love of Christ filling our hearts, we *will* change the world.

We cannot change the world if there is a lack of love within the doors of the church. When we tear down rather than build up, we must admit that we have failed in the gospel we preach.

Making God's Name Trivial

Couldn't the same be said about trivializing the name of God? We've all heard the expressions: "The man upstairs," "the big guy in the sky," or "Holy Joe" in heaven.

We come up with all these names that must be an absolute insult to God. He is not the big guy. He isn't the Holy Joe. He is God. He said to the Israelites: "I expect you to hold Me in reverence in our relationship. I am God, not man. I am the Holy One in your midst."

We trivialize God by taking His name and attaching it to ordinary swearing, which is unworthy of Him.

Remember what Jesus said in the Sermon on the Mount? He said for us not to make any kind of oath in our normal business practices (Matthew 5:33–37). I don't think He was talking about when we go to a courtroom.

Jesus was saying, "Let your yes be yes, and your no be no" (Matthew 5:37, paraphrased). If we practice calling God's name by names unworthy of Him, we attach His name to what is less than His holy nature and less than the holiness He expects of His people.

When I was a college professor, I insisted students call me by my title rather than by my first name. I was Dr. Coker. Always that. Why? Because I'm so great? No. It was because I stood in a position of authority that needed to be respected.

I think that is one of the breakdowns in our schools and our society today. We don't give consideration to the person in an honorable position. Professor. President. What disturbs me most about what's happening in our nation today is that we don't even respect the *office* of President of the United States, simply because we don't like or agree with the *person* holding the office.

But what about God? Do we treat Him as God? Or do we trivialize Him? Do we make Him a casual God? Is He the God of our spare time? Is He the God we can call upon when we need Him, but we never talk to Him except when we want something?

Is He the God I confess with my lips, but it never costs me anything? Or is He the God I confess when it costs me everything? Is He the God I can praise in church but ignore during the whole week?

God said you will not make my name foolish. You will not make my name empty. You will not make my name trivial or casual. You will not make my name syncretistic when you join it with something else. I am God. The Holy One in your midst.

This is the God before whom we bow as we worship Him.

God's Word Is Good

I've said before that the words God spoke to Israel were words of endearment rather than commandment. If we take the third word from a negative prohibition and state it as positive, we would see something more along the lines of this:

"You shall take My name earnestly."

"You shall only take My name sincerely. You shall use My name truthfully, honestly. I am God. And My name is holy. And you will take it in a way that is becoming of holiness."

Shouldn't this make us want to know God? To be in relationship and love Him? Not simply to know His name as Yahweh, but to know Him. We should want to love God with our whole heart, mind, soul, and strength. Our hearts should confess, "Not my will but His; not my glory but His; not my kingdom but His." I suggest we think about this third word in terms not only of prohibitions, but also of its positive assertions for our lives.

What's in a name? There is so much in this third word that relates to how we live. I pray that as we think about this, we remember God will not hold us guiltless if we have abused His name in our words, in our conduct, and in our heart's condition. Instead, we should confess our failure, seek forgiveness, and ask Him to cleanse our hearts and help us change. As people of the Word, we want to live by honoring God's name.

WORKBOOK

Chapter Three Questions

Question: What do you want your name—your reputation—to represent? What associations do people have with your family's name? When you commit to something or give your endorsement, does that inspire confidence in others? Has anyone ever tried to tarnish your good name, and if so, how did that affect you?

_____

_____

_____

_____

_____

_____

_____

_____

Question: Give examples of how a Christian could profane God's name with his or her conduct or attitudes. How do people sometimes try to mix the worship of the true God with idolatry? Have you tried to live both God's way and the world's way at the same time? Ask God to show you specific areas where you need to repent of taking His name in vain.

_____

_____

_____

_____

_____

_____

_____

_____

_____

_____

Question: How do you speak about God? Do you show the honor and worship that is due to Him, or do you speak flippantly or with jesting? Can God trust you to bear His name?

_____

_____

_____

_____

_____

_____

_____

_____

_____

_____

_____

Action: Do a study on the phrase "the name of the Lord" and "the name of Jesus" in Scripture and journal what you learn from your findings. Additionally, study the various names of God, and what each of them means, in understanding His character.

Prayer: Lord God, we are mindful that You love us and have called us into a covenant relationship with You. The beautiful fact is that You know us by name. We are not guiltless, for we have used Your name in ways that profane Your holiness. More frequently than we'd like to admit, we've tried to fit You into what we want. We pray for You to cleanse our hearts, establish us in newness, and remind us to live as children of God before a world that does not know You. May we represent who You are and what You have called us to be. In Jesus' name we pray. Amen.

Chapter Three Notes

CHAPTER FOUR

The Fourth Word:
Keep the Sabbath Day Holy

Remember the Sabbath day by keeping it holy. Six days you shall labor and do all your work, but the seventh day is a sabbath to the LORD your God.

—Exodus 20:8–10a *NIV*

What a tremendous word we find as the fourth word. Here, God stresses the importance of rest in our lives, a day set apart for worship. God sees that work and time each play a significant role in the true purpose of Sabbath rest—to recognize God's sovereignty.

It's important to note that the fourth word from God is *not* saying that having a strong work ethic is terrible and that we need to stop occasionally to catch our breath. Work is a good thing; it has its place and God specifically designed it to be an integral piece of our lives.

If we do much reading on the subject of the Sabbath, we will notice that people tend to take a psychological or practical approach to this word.

The psychological approach says that every individual needs to set aside a time to stop and re-collect themselves. We need time to get away from busy activities and to re-focus on what counts. Work is wonderful if we enjoy it, but the day of rest—a time when we can put all thoughts of labor aside and enjoy a time of re-creation—is vital to our overall mental, physical, and emotional health.

A word to students: during all the years of my under-graduate and graduate studies, I practiced Sunday as the day that belonged to the Lord. I needed a time when I could get away and refresh myself and I gained much from that practical observation.

A practical view of the Sabbath is a picture of the rhythmic pattern of life. You have times when you are awake and when you are asleep. You need both. If you don't sleep, the waking hours suffer the consequences. You may work hard, but if you don't have an appropriate amount of rest, then the work suffers. Everyone needs a day for personal inventory. Every family benefits from a day to renew relationships. This viewpoint isn't specifically biblical, but it makes good sense. We do need this kind of variation in our lives in order to make the most of the time we are given in this life.

Linear Versus Cyclical Time

The ancient Israelites' concept of time differed quite radically from the nations around them, as well as from the cultures and religions of today. In Israel, they considered time from a linear perspective: there is a beginning of time and an end of time. The nations around Israel, however, looked at time cyclically, because they thought of time in terms of nature. What has come before will come again, which is why it was easy for Solomon to write that there was nothing new under the sun. It's easy for us who also live in a culture that looks at time through a cyclical lens, to understand what Solomon meant.

At the time God met with Israel, they had no clocks or calendars. The world viewed time as the rising and setting of the sun. When spring came, it was time to sow the crops. Then came summer when the crops grew, and the fall when they harvested crops. With winter came a time of dormancy, which is also when people took time to rest. So, in these cultures, all of life followed the pattern of the four seasons: spring, summer, fall, and winter.

Even today, as people get older, we say they are in the winter of their lives. Time seems to ebb and flow like the cycles of the earth. Because life, in this viewpoint, is based on a never-ending cycle, time isn't considered as a precious commodity. Rather, it's an inevitability.

When God set the boundaries for the Israelites and their use of time, He showed them that time is not inconsequential, but extremely important. It's as important for us today as it was for Israel to recognize that God who created time is providently at work in His world in a linear fashion. He began His work with creation, and He will bring His work to completion on the day of Christ's return.

In the same way, we are to see our lives as linear. When we move forward into the New Testament to Hebrews 4, we see that, like everything God has established, the

Sabbath rest is about more than taking a day off from work. We have a day when our life on this earth began, and we have a day when our life on this earth will end. It doesn't make any difference how much money we have, when time runs out, all the money in the world cannot buy any of us more time. According to the author of Hebrews, there will come a time of Sabbath rest when we reach the conclusion for all human life. For believers, that end comes as our eternal rest with God in heaven. Unfortunately, not everyone will enter into that rest.

A Time for Work

Sometimes, people who do not know the Lord feel that life is rather monotonous, that it seems to be going nowhere. For the person who knows God and is a follower of the Lord Jesus Christ, that ought not be true. We should have a sense of beginning in our lives, not simply birth, but new birth. From that point, life ought to be a developing process that has a beginning, a middle, and an end, as Paul said in his prayer over the Philippian church: "I am sure of this, that he who began a good work in you will bring it to completion at the day of Jesus Christ" (Philippians 1:6).

I think God's work in us keeps life from being dull and boring. We are in the process of becoming. And as followers of Jesus Christ, we haven't reached the pinnacle yet. There is still more out there. Even on one's dying day, the statement on our lips ought to be "the best is yet to be."[23] As believers, we can be assured that there is more, because God has set life on a course, and He invites us to "come further up and further in" as Reepicheep says in C. S. Lewis's book *The Last Battle*.[24]

So often in other religions, people see themselves caught in their humanity with the only way out being a mystical, meditative process of escape from whatever is holding them in bondage. So, a holy man in his religion may sit and stare all day long with the hope that, somehow, he can escape the bonds of life and ultimately reach the state of pure spirit. He waits for nirvana where he will arrive being totally absorbed into the spirit that is his god.

That is not a biblical concept at all. Life is not monotonous. The Israelites did not feel like they were trapped in the human circumstances of life.[25] The attitude of Scripture is not that work traps us in misery, but rather that it is an experience of God's grace and love. And if we are walking in His paths of righteousness then, indeed, whatever work we do in this life is a part of the process of becoming all God has designed us to be.

The Fullness of Sabbath

Remember the Sabbath day, to keep it holy. Six days you shall labor, and do all your work, but the seventh day is a Sabbath to the LORD your God. On it you shall not do any work, you, or your son, or your daughter, your male servant, or your female servant, or your livestock, or the sojourner who is within your gates. For in six days the LORD made heaven and earth, the sea, and all that is in them, and rested on the seventh day. Therefore the LORD blessed the Sabbath day and made it holy.

—Exodus 20:8–11

Observe the Sabbath day, to keep it holy, as the Lord your God commanded you. Six days you shall labor and do all your work, but the seventh day is a Sabbath to the Lord your God. On it you shall not do any work, you or your son or your daughter or your male servant or your female servant, or your ox or your donkey or any of your livestock, or the so-journer who is within your gates, that your male servant and your female servant may rest as well as you. You shall remember that you were a slave in the land of Egypt, and the Lord your God brought you out from there with a mighty hand and an outstretched arm. Therefore the Lord your God commanded you to keep the Sabbath day.
—Deuteronomy 5:12–15

If we look at what God told Israel about the Sabbath in Exodus and Deuteronomy, we notice a difference that occurs between these two passages of Scripture. We see theological tones. In the book of Exodus, the reason for the Sabbath is that God created everything that is part of the world in six time periods. But in the seventh time period He rested. That doesn't mean He was tired. The word in Hebrew, *šābat*, means God ceased from His work.[26] He stopped. That's what this commandment is about.

In Genesis, chapters 1 and 2, we read that God created man in His image—both male and female. He never explains in Genesis 1 what that image is. He only says that man shall have dominion over the rest of creation, so God tasked Adam with naming all of the creatures of earth.

Adam and Eve, being in the image of God, were given the right to exercise dominion over creation. But then comes the seventh day. And note that the first use of the word *holy,* as we see it in the Bible, is found in this passage in Genesis where God said that He set apart the seventh day, and He called it "holy" (Genesis 2:3).

Everything that is called holy belongs to God, which God reminded Israel when He established the Sabbath day in the book of Exodus. He invited them to pause long enough in their week to remember that God is sovereign over all that exists. And He invites us, through this fourth word, to do the same.

God created you in His image. He has made you in His likeness. He has created you in such a way that you can exercise dominion over all creation. *But* once a week you are to stop and remember you are not the ultimate sovereign. You are not God. You are only created in the image of God. Thus you need to stop on that day and recognize that there is One more sovereign than yourself.

Do you ever stop to wonder why so much emphasis is laid upon the Sabbath day in the Hebrew Bible? This is not because it's a ritual, but there are theological undercurrents. God was saying through His prophets that the day you forget the Sabbath is the day you introduce destruction into the nation. There is nothing mystical about a day, but the truth of that day is essential to life. If you forget that God is the ultimate sovereign, then you will mess up the rest of the days, too.

Deuteronomy looks at the Sabbath a little differently. As slaves in Egypt, there was no time of rest for them. The Sabbath was a reminder that they were once slaves in Egypt, but God delivered them out of bondage, making them His redeemed people. So, once every week they were to stop and remember specifically that in His grace He made them a free people.

In the same way, we have been redeemed out of the

bondage of sin through Christ's death and resurrection. For us, the Sabbath is a reminder to stop and praise God that His grace has been extended to our lives, giving us freedom and eternal life.

The Sabbath is a holy day because it belongs to God and because we belong to God. In Exodus we belong to God because of creation, and in Deuteronomy we belong to God by right of redemption. God has made us His own. This use of time is not inconsequential and goes far beyond our view of time, whether cyclical or linear. It flows right into the way we live our lives and the way we see ourselves as His creation through His redemption.

Contemporary Setting

A change happened after Jesus was resurrected on the third day (which was the first day of the week). The church began to develop an emphasis of observing the Lord's Day not on the seventh day, but on the first day. Originally the disciples, as did Jesus, went to the synagogue every week on the seventh day. They continued the pattern, as we see in the book of Acts. They made no break with what had been and what Jesus had taught them about worshiping God.

When the apostle John wrote the revelation God gave him of the final days, it seems that the Sabbath is made lesser and the Lord's Day becomes greater (Revelation 1:10). Somewhere during the time when John wrote Revelation, the Lord's Day, or the first day of the week, became the day when the believers came together before God to praise Him. It was not only because Jesus was resurrected, but because we too have been resurrected into newness of life (Romans 6:4–5).

Early on, worship became a celebration where believers rejoiced in Jesus' resurrection and in the believer's resurrection from the death of sin into the life of the Spirit. On that day they would receive communion, recognizing the presence of Jesus in their lives and rejoicing in what He has done.

It wasn't until AD 321 that Emperor Constantine made the decision that Christianity would be the official religion of the Roman Empire, and what would become the Holy Roman Empire. Even though there were all kinds of religions around in the empire at the time, Christianity would be their chief religion. Constantine issued an edict in a legal statement that the day of worship would be the first day of the week and also created a list of activities you could and could not do on that day. Many of the strict Sunday observances that are still held today come from this set of "blue laws."[27]

As the Sabbath changed to the first day of the week, to Sunday, our view of what the Sabbath is and what it should look like, has changed as well.

Assault on the Bible

The Bible reveals God's relationship with us. As God revealed more about His nature and His plan, people began to record those experiences. Over time, some Jewish scholars developed the theory that the Ten Commandments were not what God had spoken, but what man had developed.

Beginning in the eighteenth century, that theory became the premise of much academic study and theological inquiry. The Bible, therefore, came under the assault of modern, higher criticism. When I went to seminary, we had to study all the issues of the higher, critical movement and students still study it in certain seminaries. Basically, this interpretation of historical events ends up being a denial that God reveals Himself in word to His people. The new way of interpreting the Bible is to say it doesn't have basic, fundamental meaning until *you* or *I* give meaning to it. I think the purpose was to undermine the truth that is the absolute word of God.

Without revelation directly from God, which is critical to the Christian faith, we would not have truth. Revelation is critical; it's not accidental. If God has not spoken to us, if God has not declared the truth to us, then all we can lean on is our own human opinions. If you can say the Bible is only the product of the human mind, immediately it ceases to be the ultimate word of truth. So, the Bible comes under assault.

Second, the church is also under assault today in terms of the day of worship. It started a long time ago, and now we find more and more encroachments on Sunday. These encroachments come from the outside by all kinds of events going on. Youth league games are scheduled on Sunday morning at the time when worship should be taking place. Even religious conferences are scheduled for Sunday. Worship is undermined. That's not accidental, for it reflects a worldly purpose and design. Revelation is vital not only to our Christian faith, but also to the worship of our God. Both are necessary to the maintenance of our spiritual lives.

Like a coal that's pulled from the fire will lose its heat, when we are isolated, we do not have the strength to maintain and sustain our faith. Jesus called His disciples to be part of a body, not as individuals, but as a people unified. Worship is vital to us. A denial of the church comes through undermining revelation *and* our worship services.

I've heard it said that there ought to be a day set apart for a people who are set apart. If indeed we are a set-apart people, we demonstrate that by setting apart a day to declare what we believe and whose we are.

When I turn to Scripture, I find that need for being set apart. In ancient Israel, it was to remind them that they were not owners, they were tenants, as we are today. "The earth is the LORD's and the fullness thereof, the world and those who dwell therein" (Psalm 24:1).

We need the time to reflect on the truth that God has made us and that we belong to Him. We need that sense of identity of who we are—as well as whose we are—and what we are about. Take away the worship service and we cut into the idea that as a people, we can make a difference in the world around us.

Church and Worship Are Key

Worship is a key part of our relationship with God. Maintaining that day apart is not the easiest thing to do because of pressures coming against us. The only way we are going to keep that day set apart is to be intentional about it. We have to be willing to be counter-cultural with a sense of passion and enthusiasm that celebrating the

Lord's Day is important. If we are not passionate about
this idea—that we have an opportunity to come together
and praise God and let our lives be a witness to our gratitude for what He has done for us—then we will come to
the place where we lose the cutting edge of our faith.
Maintaining worship is not easy. We must stand against a
world that says we can do something else on Sunday
mornings. We make a choice, don't we?

I remember when I was a sophomore at Tulane University in New Orleans, Louisiana. The District Superinten-
dent (D.S.) of the United Methodist Church asked if I
would serve a little church that didn't have a pastor. I accepted that invitation and began preaching to those people. We had a good time worshiping there, and I began
learning how to be a pastor.

During that time, the conference considered starting
another church. The D.S. wanted me to go to another community and take a survey of the people. So, I did. I remember one man in particular. I went into his place of business,
telling him our intentions, wanting to know if he would be
interested in being part of a new church. He looked at me
and said, "The Masonic lodge is my church."

Don't misunderstand me. I am not throwing stones at
Masons. But a church is more than a gathering of like-
minded people. For over two thousand years, the church
has declared, "Yes, we worship the Lord our God, and we
belong to Him."

The thriving body of believers must be willing to declare this message despite any threats against us. Despite
mockery. Despite persecution. This is why our worship
services should be vibrant and meaningful. If we simply

go through the motions of showing up at a specific time and place and then returning to our lives as if we are no different than the rest of the world, then what is the difference between us and the Rotary Club? Why should anybody care?

But if there is a God who created us, a Christ who has redeemed us, and an eternity that awaits us, we ought to be excited about that! There should be an intensity in you and me. If we are not intense about worship, then what is our message to the world?

I love to hear churches sing loudly their praises to God so that others may hear. Let them hear, "Holy, holy, holy! Lord God Almighty," and, "What a Friend We Have in Jesus." In a weary and chaotic world, they need such a message of hope.

Of course, it's not as easy as I am stating it. Worship has changed from the era of the Old Testament to New Testament times. And it is changing today.

This is the Day

We live in an industrial society where industries cannot shut down on Sundays. Steel mills must keep those furnaces roaring on Sunday, as well as any other day. Hospitals cannot be shut down on Sunday. If a house catches fire, no one wants the fire department to be completely shut down.

In today's culture, I think it is going to become more and more difficult to keep Sunday as it used to be. So, the question is, what alternatives are we ready to suggest for our day? For the nurse who must work in the hospital on

Sunday, are we ready to offer another time for worship? Are we willing to remain as fluid as the early disciples were and be ready to meet the needs in people's lives? We could be rigid and say: If you cannot worship on Sunday, that is your tough luck. But if we do that, it will not honor the Lord.

I find it interesting that Jesus specifically told his followers to set apart a day of the week to worship God. He never said worship me on the first day of the week. He never said it must be this day and not another. The apostle Paul, who authored the bulk of the New Testament, said some honor one day over another, but others see every day alike (Romans 14:5).

We live in a world where lives are in flux. Contrary to the Pharisees with their 1,521 prohibitions for the Sabbath day,[28] God never intended for the Sabbath to be a day of oppression. Rather, He gave it one positive note: wholeness and rest come when we worship Him.

Take the time to remember that He is God and we are His people, and Jesus Christ is our Lord and Redeemer who was raised from the dead on the third day. He ascended to heaven and one day He is coming back again.

As Christians this is an exciting time. We have an opportunity to make our stand for Christ in such a way that we bear witness to Christ, who has made the ultimate difference in our lives. I think we can challenge the hungry hearts of people as we open our hearts and doors of the church in a more flexible way.

We need to counteract the enchantment of this present world around us. We need to establish and protect a time away from the demands on us so we can rid ourselves of the influence of the world and fix our eyes on Christ.

We need church because we need one another. I personally value being part of a body of worshipers of Christ who come around in those times when I need encouragement and have to deal with my own feelings and faults, and those times when stress comes, and I can find the strength I'm lacking in another brother or sister in Christ. And you need members of the body of Christ for the same reasons.

We need to worship, to praise our Lord Jesus Christ with all of our heart, mind, soul, and strength. We need worship services where we come as believers to praise Him and rejoice in what He has done for us.

The fourth word tells us to remember the Sabbath and to keep it holy. When we do so, we keep ourselves holy. When we forget, it's at our own peril.

Remember God has created you and has redeemed you, and by His grace He has given you time to experience His presence.

WORKBOOK

Chapter Four Questions

Question: "God's work in us is what keeps life from being dull and boring." What work is God doing in your life right now? How (and what) are you becoming? How are you joining with God's work in your life through participation in His transformation?

_____

_____

_____

_____

_____

_____

_____

_____

_____

Question: How can observing a Sabbath in your life help you to specifically remember God's *sovereignty* and His *redemption*? How can you better incorporate these themes into your rest and worship?

_____

_____

_____

_____

_____

_____

_____

_____

_____

_____

_____

Question: What are the main competitors for your time and attention on Sundays? What changes could you make and what commitments would be necessary to make church a priority and worship a habit in your life?

_____

_____

_____

_____

_____

_____

_____

_____

_____

_____

_____

Action: Brainstorm with a group of fellow believers about ways that you can honor the Sabbath in the current culture. How can the church help those who have to work on Sundays? How can parents of young children, emergency personnel, or church staff members experience a true day of rest and worship? How can you enjoy the Lord's Day and make it a holy (set-apart) day without becoming legalistic?

Prayer: Our Father, we thank You for the beauty of our sanctuaries where we worship and praise You. In many parts of the world, they don't have beautiful churches. Yet, in these humble settings, people come to praise You in languages we don't understand as they gather to sing, pray, and listen to Your Word. They come with thankful hearts, as do we. May we all resolve to love and worship You in the beauty of holiness. In Christ's name we pray. Amen.

Chapter Four Notes

_____

_____

_____

_____

_____

_____

_____

_____

_____

_____

_____

_____

_____

_____

_____

_____

_____

_____

_____

_____

CHAPTER FIVE

The Fifth Word:
Honor Your Parents

Honor your father and your mother, that your days may be long in the land that the LORD your God is giving you.
—Exodus 20:12

When we look at the fifth word, we see a slight shift in focus. Where the first four words direct our attention to God's place in our lives, in our speech, and in our worship, the fifth word looks to the significance of the family. It would be easy to say the fifth word marks a break, but when we look at it more closely in terms of the first four words, we find a natural progression taking place. In order to see that progression more clearly, let's take a quick look back at the previous words God spoke.

The first word tells how we should honor God with all our heart, soul, and might (Deuteronomy 6:5). We are to remember there is only one God, and besides Him there is no other. He is our creator, so we are responsible and accountable to Him.

In the second word, God tells something about Himself. He is not to be replaced by the likeness of any part of creation. God is not human, neither is He anything like His creation. He stands above it. He is not identified with anything within it, because He has created it all.

In the third word God says we are to give reverence to His name. We are to honor and respect who He is, and if we do that, then we will discover "I AM" is present with us. But, as we read in Ezekiel, if we profane God's name as the Israelites did, we are going to discover it brings judgment on the land as well as the people living in the land (Ezekiel 36:23).

The fourth word shows us how to worship God. The focus of this word is about setting aside a time for remembrance that He is God and we are not. It's about remembering who God is and what He has done (freeing us from bondage). He is our redeemer.

He has invited us into a close, personal relationship with Him. It is in that invitation of relationship that we see the natural flow from the words that came before to the words that come after.

The Importance of Family

Honor your father and your mother, as the LORD your God commanded you, that your days may be long, and that it may go well with you in the land that the LORD your God is giving you.
—Deuteronomy 5:16

While the first four commandments deal with God as our creator, the fifth word deals with God's co-creators: fathers and mothers. They are those who have the opportunity to participate in God's creation. That reminds us our lives are a gift, not only from God but also from our earthly parents. In the first word, we learn that God created us in His image. This fifth word is a reminder that we are not self-made. Our parents have participated in creation, for God has allowed them to be a part of His work.

The grace that God gives by original creation and by the act of redemption is received not only from our Creator God but also from our earthly parents. We are graced-people. More than we realize. We are people of grace because there were those who cared for us when we could not care for ourselves. They changed our diapers when we could not do so. They fed us when we could not provide for ourselves. They protected us when we did not know anything about protection. They were present even before we asked. Grace is a part of life from God *and* from those we call mother and father. It's arrogant to claim independence as though we are free from relationships with others.

Therefore, there is an expected response from us, a response of gratitude that ought to be written indelibly across the pages of our lives. This involves responsibility and accountability, for we have a debt to pay; and that's not a popular thought today.

First, let's look again at the order of these words. If the fifth word follows logically from the first four, then the fifth word precedes logically everything that comes after it. Some call the words that follow: the "second tablet of the Law." That is to say, before men and women can enjoy the benefits of society, they must begin with their relationships within the home.

The next set of commandments—thou shall not kill, thou shall not steal, thou shall not commit adultery, thou shall not bear false witness, and thou shall not covet—all flow out of the relationship first established in the home. It is the very foundation on which all the other words from God are built.

A Message to Adults

Children, obey your parents in the Lord, for this is right. "Honor your father and mother" (this is the first commandment with a promise), "that it may go well with you and that you may live long in the land." Fathers, do not provoke your children to anger, but bring them up in the discipline and instruction of the Lord.
—Ephesians 6:1–4

When you look at the words God spoke in Exodus and Deuteronomy, it's important that we look to whom God was speaking. This word is spoken not to children, but to adults. Paul, in Ephesians 6, when addressing the relationships within in the home, begins with addressing children, but then makes it a point to address the fathers.

I believe it's significant we understand this word was first addressed to adults. That has some implications for us as we think about the responsibility we have. As we look at what God has given to the Israelites as His people, and as we look at our own society, we must realize that the principles of society are not established by our children *but by the adults.* Children follow along what adults have already set for them by example.

Today we have become critical of young people, as if somehow they invented our world and set the patterns by which we live. We must stop and understand that their actions are derived from the activities and attitudes of adults.

But there's more to this, for God speaks to the adults first. He's reminding them to show reverence to those who came before them, who were older and possibly unable to care for themselves anymore.

God is reminding us that as our parents cared for us when we were children and could not fend for ourselves, it is our responsibility to care for the elderly in our families. We are to make sure their individual needs are met, for we owe them a tremendous debt. And in honoring them, we teach our children to honor us and the Lord whom we serve.

Child Development

Second, I call your attention to when this commandment was given. Hebrew culture had only one means to develop the lives of children and that was within the family. They did not have a government, because they were basically a wandering tribe. They did not have other institutions that are part of our society today, such as schools. God called their attention to the family as the only instrument they possessed to prepare society for the years ahead.

I want to assure you that this concept is not simply for the Hebrew culture then, because the importance of family is still first and foremost in God's view.

As the family is, so society will be. We are looking around and asking questions: What's happening to us today? Why are these terrible changes taking place? Who's responsible for it all? We may seek to lay the blame for our decline at several different doorsteps, but ultimately it comes back to the decline of the family.

It's time for us to go back to this fifth word and ask: God, what are you saying to us today? The family today is no less formative and foundational as it was when God gave the commandments.

Honor Is Heavy

The third detail I want you to notice is that the Hebrew does not use the word *obey*. It uses the Hebrew word *kābēd*, which means "honor."[29] This word indicates heaviness. It is a word used in one form of the noun to describe the liver in your body.[30] It is one of those unseemly organs that Paul talks about in 1 Corinthians 12:23, that heavy object in the middle of your torso, often overlooked and yet crucial to your entire being.

It seems to me what God is saying to the Israelites (and to us) is that we need to take seriously the matter of the family. Family is not an inconsequential fact in life. It is one of those heavy, weighted systems because of its significance. Take it seriously. Give family the honored place it deserves in our lives. If we do that, God says it will be well with us, and our lives will be long in the land. If we forget this, then we discover we have ignored something weighty and significant for life, and we don't live well without it.

Kābēd is also the word for *glory*.[31] It's a word used to talk about glorifying God. We glorify God, because God is not insignificant. He is the most significant One concerning life. When we honor family, we honor Him. We put God in the place where we take Him seriously. And we put the family in the place where we take it seriously, because God has given us this means of perpetuating ourselves and our society.

Statement to Society

The promise reads: Do this so "that your days may be long, and that it may go well with you in the land that the LORD your God is giving you" (Deuteronomy 5:16). I think it is safe to say this is not a promise made to individuals, but to the people as a whole.

It is not something that comes across as: Well, if you obey your mother and father when you are a child, and if you honor your parents as you grow older, then you are going to live to be 95. This is not a promise for length of days to an individual, but rather it is a statement to a society. We do this not so we may personally live a long life, but so our culture itself might survive.

In her book, *Smoke on the Mountain,* Joy Davidman makes a statement I think is interesting. It captures what all of us have said one way or another. She wrote: "...society that destroys the family destroys itself."[32]

I do not think that is debatable. God says it in this fifth word. If we want our society to survive, then it means we must take seriously this weighty matter of the family. We give it due regard, which means we focus our concerns upon the family as the significant formative instrument God designed it to be. God loved us so much He placed us in families, and that's as important in our own day as it was in the day God spoke to Israel in the desert.

Contemporary Responsibility

Whatever life might have been among the Israelites, my primary interest is the contemporary observations you and I make as we think of what God says about the significance of the family. We can begin immediately to identify the flags of danger all around us in our time.

For example, let's take the flag of strong individualism emphasized in our day when the key word is not responsibility but rights. It's when the key idea is not dependence but rather that I am my own person. I have the right to do what I want. Whatever good American individualism may contribute, too often it also brings with it a focus on self that ends up ultimately destroying the very ideal we want to keep. Today's emphasis upon our rights destroys responsibility.

In our society, we know what's harmful to our bodies, but we have disregarded personal responsibility in staying away from many harmful substances. We have been warned about drugs, alcohol, and cigarettes, but ignore the dangers. When we do not want to carry responsibility, we lay the blame upon someone else.

What disturbs me is the accepted idea that someone else is responsible for our choices, and thus lawsuits are filed. We say we have our rights, which free us of our responsibility. As we rear our children, we emphasize individualism and thus begin to see the deterioration of the sense of authority.

A long time ago, I picked up one of John R. W. Stott's books on preaching. It set forth the idea of being between two worlds.[33] The pastor has a responsibility of standing between God's heavenly kingdom and our own contemporary world. Stott dedicated several pages to the idea that one of the characteristics of our day is that we have undermined the sense of authority.

People wonder what has happened to our schools. One of the answers is we have undermined authority to the point that children have no sense of responsibility toward those placed over them. Today it's the teachers' fault and not the children.

But if students do not accept any sense of authority, then they are not amenable to learning. It is frustrating to teach people who are not open to being taught. The attitude of "what I think is good enough" is an accepted expression. That results in a breakdown regarding authority and the willingness to place oneself under another to be instructed.

This attitude comes from adults as well. Often, adults fail to give the respect and honor due to those in authority over us. The highest authority to some these days is their own opinion. Anyone who says anything that conflicts with their set opinion is viewed as an enemy or someone who is not worthy of respect. This is especially true when it comes to the gaps between different generations.

Once, while at the airport, I saw a man who had to be in his sixties. He was dressed as if he were eighteen and looked like something out of a circus. We have idolized youthfulness and failed to understand how beautiful age is. Age brings values that youth don't possess.

What's puzzling, however, is that as obsessed as we are with youthfulness, we have forgotten the value of children. For many, children are an interference—they keep us from realizing what we want to do. However, the psalmist wrote: "Behold, children are a heritage from the LORD, the fruit of the womb a reward. Like arrows in the hand of a warrior are the children of one's youth" (Psalm 127:3–4).

Today the attitude seems to be: You are blessed if you do not have any kids to get in the way. Consequently, we discover the lack of honoring our children produces a mentality that causes young people to feel, not only unappreciated, but valueless and unwanted.

Who is to blame?

Perhaps we are asking the wrong question. We ask why kids are involved in high school shootings and illegal drugs, and we demand more accountability and harsher criminal charges against those on whom we place the blame.

Maybe we need to look at ourselves and the matter of our hearts. The real answer is that we have allowed the home to deteriorate. We have forsaken God's fifth word, and in so doing, we have produced young people who do not know how to keep the last five words God gave.

President George W. Bush once observed that "good and evil are present in this world, and between the two there can be no compromise."[34] It's not only that moral evil is evident in the world, but the problem begins right in the home with those of us who are parents. It begins in churches with those of us who are models for children, and in society as teachers, or anyone else who has the responsibility of being parental figures for children. If we cannot learn to honor and respect those placed in authority over us in our families, we will never be able to resolve other major issues in our world.

The Post-Industrial Family

While working toward his doctorate in psychology, a friend of mine studied the effects of industrialization on the maturity of children. He discovered that industrialization has created what we call adolescence; it didn't exist prior to the industrial revolution in western civilization. Prior to that era, children were considered adults when they reached the age of sixteen.

In America, and other post-industrial nations, sixteen-year-olds are still children. Not only are they not mature enough to start their own lives, they're not equipped with the skills to do so. We tell them that if they want to be able to support themselves or a family, they have to finish high school and go on to college. Then we say that a college degree is not enough. They should get a master's degree if they're going to get ahead or earn a specialized title behind their name.

So, young adults put off marriage longer and longer, if they ever get married at all. And we wonder why they're so frustrated and why their hormones are raging out of control. This is not the world my father grew up in. I loved to listen to his stories of how they went to church riding in the back of their wagon. But that is not my world, nor is it yours. We live in an industrialized and technological society that has not only changed young people, it has changed marriage.

During the agricultural era, dads worked on a farm and were always with their families. Dads involved the kids whether they were hoeing, plowing, or reaping. When moms got ready to make preserves, the family got involved. With industrialization, dads left the home. With the Second World War, moms left the home. Now, they have totally different worlds, and their lives are like ships passing in the night.

People say there is something wrong with marriage today. That is true. Part of it is created by a culture that is now industrialized. Don't write that off too quickly, because the changes that are happening in our world are affecting us. Sometimes, in our Christian faith, we have been slow to change with the culture that's changing all around us. We have been content to say, "Look what the devil is doing," as though we do not have any responsibility for what is going on around us.

We could highlight government intrusion that mandates children ought to be free of their parents in many respects. That concept moves them from parental constraint, but it does not free them from governmental restraint. We live in a world where the media has identified the kids as their prime market, not the eighteen-year-old, but those as young as twelve.

Market managers know that if the twelve-year-olds don't have their own money, their parents will give it to them. Industry has now made the kids the object of their materialism, knowing they can make more money that way. Teen magazine ads say things like, "If your mom doesn't understand you, write to us. We will give you sane advice."

Time to Invest

God has a word for us. The word is: "Honor your father and your mother" (Exodus 20:12). That word begins with us as adults. We are the ones who set the pattern. By our attitude toward our own parents, we teach our children what their attitude should be toward us. We are the ones responsible for the breakdown of authority, obedience, and respect within the home. God says: "If you want your culture to survive, if you want life to continue, you better reassess what you are doing in the home."

Here is my word for us. You and I need to stop and look at ourselves and ask: How do we begin to be the solution? As parents who still have children at home, it means we need to look at the patterns we are setting, the attitudes we are conveying, the expectations and responsibility we are willing to accept. Also, consider the respect we give our children as we understand they live in a changing world, and as we give them room to develop and godly wisdom to navigate the challenges they face.

If we do not have children of our own at home, we begin by paying attention to the children in our church. Try to spend time talking with them. They are our future. You and I need to invest ourselves in them. If they are only rug-rats under our feet, if they are only troublesome teens, we have set the course of our future, and it is not good.

May God help us to take inventory and start again looking seriously at what God expects of us. "God setteth the solitary in families" (Psalm 68:6 KJV). When we honor family, we honor God.

WORKBOOK

Chapter Five Questions

Question: How can parents create an environment that teaches and models the concept of honoring parents and motivates children to do so? What sort of parenting (or lack thereof) makes it difficult for a son or daughter to honor a parent? If you have children, do they feel wanted, loved, and nurtured in your home?

_____

_____

_____

_____

_____

_____

_____

_____

_____

Question: Whom or what do you look to as responsible for societal ills such as poverty, racism, divorce, drug abuse, abortion, teen depression and suicide, and casual sex? How can each of these things be traced back to an overall breakdown of the family unit? As a parent, do you shift responsibility for your children's training to the church or school? How can these institutions help parents in their God-ordained jobs and how might they hinder them?

_____

_____

_____

_____

_____

_____

_____

_____

_____

_____

_____

Question: What is your attitude toward authority? Do you show respect for those in positions of leadership in the government, church, and workplace? If your children honored you in the same way that you honor those in authority over you, would they be obeying this commandment?

Action: Read a book or take a course on biblical parenting. Study trends among teens regarding social media usage and the particular temptations they are facing in this generation. Talk to pre-teens and teens about the struggles in their lives and what they need from their parents and leaders. Apply what you learn to your own home. If you do not have children at home, how can you come alongside the parents in your church to help them fulfill their role, and how can you encourage the young people in your church to honor their parents?

Prayer: Lord God, we don't believe that any of the ten words You gave to the Israelites were inconsequential.

Only ten words, and one has to do with the family, as fundamental and basic to everything else. Lord, cause us to evaluate our families—to look at ourselves and ask the important questions. Father God, would You teach us about the value we place on our families, what patterns we set? How do we give time for our children, our own and others? We pray that You will bring us and our society back to a life-long concern for our families. We ask in Christ's name. Amen.

Chapter Five Notes

CHAPTER SIX

The Sixth Word: Life Belongs to God

Thou shalt not kill.
—*Exodus 20:13* KJV

Like the fifth word, the sixth word shows a shift in focus. The first four words reveal what our relationship with God should look like. The fifth word shows us what our relationship with family should look like. And the sixth word (along with the remaining words) shows us what our society should look like.

As we've already established in the previous chapter, when we're in a right relationship with God and our families honor one another, our society will thrive, and our lives will be blessed. Can we imagine such a society? For one, lives would be so highly respected that there would be no murder, no adultery, no stealing, no slandering, and no envying the gifts God has given one another.

Imagine what a world would be like if there were no such thing as killing. As desirable as the idea of no killing may be, Scripture tells us the truth about the sinfulness of our hearts that continues to dream up and execute the kind of violence that disheartens, discourages, and destroys what we call society. When Jesus described His second coming, He said that "you will hear of wars and rumors of wars" (Matthew 24:6). Hostility and acts of violence—so much a part of our news—permeate the record of human history in a horrendous way.

The sixth word, "Thou shalt not kill," is simply stated. Along with the next two words, these are all pointed, terse, succinct statements: "Thou shalt not." This seems clear, but we find ourselves struggling with what does this mean and how do we apply it.

While many Bibles translate the sixth word as, "You shall not commit murder," the Hebrew word used here is *rāṣaḥ*, which means "kill."[35]

This is important to note, because where the word *rāṣaḥ* has a broader application, the word for *murder* is restricted in its meaning. *Murder/murderer* occurs infrequently in the Old Testament, so it's a relatively rare word. In Numbers 35, the Hebrew word *rāṣaḥ* is used to denote manslaughter (accidental) rather than homicide (premeditated). In this portion of the Law, provision was made that allowed a person responsible for an accidental death to flee to a refuge city, where his life would be spared.

As you look at the term *rāṣaḥ* and try to follow its use in Scripture, you find other Hebrew words for kill or murder that do not apply to this sixth word, "Thou shalt not kill" (Exodus 20:13 KJV). Scholars have tried to come to a definitive term, and they have debated about motives. The clearest definition I have come across is simply to say that the sixth word refers to *taking a life without the right or authority to do so.*

A Common Community

My concern here is not only looking at the Hebrew text and dissecting the words. My goal is to bring the meaning of God's words into our contemporary setting and explore how they apply to our lives today.

If you go back to the text, God is giving the Israelites boundaries by which they can perform His will and be His people. God is speaking of a positive and a negative all in one word. He is setting before the people the compass for their lives—if you live in this way, society will prosper and you will benefit from living in such a land; if you fail to live in this way, society will collapse and you will not benefit from living in such a land.

Taking a life doesn't just go against God, who alone is the author of life; it goes against the covenant community. The covenant the Israelites made with God did not exist in isolation from their relationship with one another but included that relationship. Because they were a covenant people, everyone within that nation was not only bound to God in covenant, they were uniquely bound to each other.

In the New Testament, there is a word used for that concept. In fact, we have commonly used it as a name for a Sunday school class. The Greek word is *koinonia*, derived from the word *koinos*, which means "common"

(Acts 2:44).[36] It was a business term used to describe partners. We can also use it to describe two people who form a relationship because they have something in common with some other person or object. In other words, because these two people have the same relationship to this third entity, they are automatically in relationship with one another. So, when you and I say Christ is our Savior, it means that we are bound together in covenant because of our common relationship with Christ.

Taking the life of another unjustly—without authority or right—not only violates the fact that God is humanity's creator, but it violates the covenant God has established with all who are in covenant with Him. God's word provided the people a guideline in terms of their relationships. It was understood from those early days that taking the life of another person was not an option in the covenant community. They were to live together in love and harmony.

Apply God's Word Today

I want now to address a question we wrestle with about this commandment God has given. Numbers 35, for example, states even manslaughter is a violation of this commandment. Even in our own society, there's a provision for accidental death.

In Hebrew society, if a person accidently killed another person, that person could flee to a refuge city and be spared from death until the evidence had been examined and judgment pronounced. Even then, they had to confront the fact that killing itself was wrong. He was not free to stay where he was. If that person left the protection of the refuge city, the person responsible for being the redeemer or avenger of the family could put that person to death with no recourse (Numbers 35:19, 35:27).

Is there anything in our own time that would make that commandment relevant and usable? Yes. Take the idea of carelessness producing homicide. Consider an automobile accident involving a fatality and the driver is declared to be at fault. That driver is charged with vehicular manslaughter and is held responsible. In the case where the driver was driving under the influence (or was an unsafe driver due to age, health, or distractions), one could easily argue that although the death was not pre-meditated, the driver knowingly put others at risk by getting behind the wheel that day.

What about a manufacturer who produces a product he knows is a potential danger to people? Yet, in disregard to that danger, the manufacturer continues to make the product available. Then some child dies as a result. Does not that have any moral consequence?

I want to look further than the question of the law. I want to look at Scripture and ask about moral responsibility. Are we to hold each other responsible when our actions (or inactions) result in the death of another? In the light of this word, I suggest the answer is "yes." When God gave this command, He was saying anything that brought death to another person could never be viewed morally inconsequential.

Negligence plays a large part in deciding this moral issue. I am responsible as I get in my automobile because it involves me in the lives of other people. Anytime I take a risk or wrongly use an instrument or my position of authority, and that action results in the damage or death of another, I am morally accountable to God for what I have done. That's the implication of this commandment if we take the word seriously.

Another question has been raised again and again. What about the use of tobacco products? We know full well (read the labels on the packages) that tobacco destroys lives. With such an uprising against the use of tobacco products in America,[37] manufacturers now want to shift the advertisements to the international community where medical warnings are not known or appreciated.[38] Morally innocent? Morally inconsequential? In the light of this commandment, I want to suggest the answer is "no." When God gave this word, He was saying anything that brought death to another person could never be viewed morally inconsequential.

Suicide

There is another question that's difficult to talk about. That is the act of suicide. It's difficult because families have been torn apart by suicide. They carry such a deep hurt in their hearts, and the last thing a pastor wants to do is put his finger into the wound. We know that suicide has brought much tragedy to many families. It is difficult to comprehend the mental state of a person who does such a thing to himself.

When we approach this subject of suicide, we must do so with gentleness and certainly with no judgmental attitude. Based on my study of Scripture, I believe that suicide is no more acceptable in the eyes of God than is the murder of another individual. Suicide is wrong, morally wrong.

How God deals with people who are in such mental states that permit them to do things, which you and I cannot conceive of in our right minds, is not for us to judge. God is the judge of each person's life, and we are not. But it is the responsibility of the church to uphold God's Word, and that includes teaching that taking one's own life is wrong in God's eyes. Both life and death are in God's hands. Paul admonished Timothy to "take hold of the eternal life to which you were called" and "to keep the commandment unstained and free from reproach" (1 Timothy 6:12, 6:14; see also Genesis 1:27 and Job 2:9–10).

Morally, as a body of Christ, we must stand against suicide and commit to God's care and judgment anyone who violates His command. And we as a covenant community must also become better about coming alongside those who are struggling with depression and thoughts of self-harm and help redirect them back toward the ultimate source of hope and life.

Assisted Suicide and Euthanasia

I want to press the point further. Not only from the standpoint of suicide, but regarding people whose lives have reached a point where society no longer views them as productive members of the community or who are facing terminal illnesses.

What does God say about persons who spend most of every day in wracking pain with little relief? Do we have the right or authority to step in and say that lives like these are not worth living, and that we need to give these persons the option to end their lives?

The great question we must first answer is: Is it ever right for us to say that a life is no longer worth living? Is there not the opportunity for human beings to suffer redemptively? Could it be that in the suffering, one finds the ability to handle life through Christ?

I once worked an Emmaus Walk where I heard a woman say she wanted to leave on Friday night. She was a cancer survivor and said she was on a different path than the other women in attendance. She felt she had nothing in common with those who had not faced death, that she was not getting anything out of what others had to say.

I asked her this one question: "Is it possible that God sent you here, not for what you could get out of this weekend, but for what you can put into it?"

Maybe the answer to suffering is not what we *get*, but what we have the opportunity to *give*. I guarantee you history is filled with stories of people who suffered grievously and, at the same time, were able to bear witness for Christ. The gospel, if it works at all, must work in the tough places and not only in the easy places.

I know this is a complicated subject without simple solutions. Medical science presents questions when it moves to preserve and sustain life in situations that in other periods of time would have been fatal.

We put people on machines that can breathe for them and apply other means to keep the body functioning. Then the question is raised: Is it morally right to take a person off life support? I confess, I don't know the answer. When people say you don't have any right to play God and take a person off the machine, my only response would be: Did they play God when they put him on the machine? Is there a place for making intelligent judgments based on the facts at hand?

When it comes to how we face our final days, these are moral questions that require us, as believers, to seek out God's wisdom. Someone may be tempted to say God spoke the words at Sinai to a primitive society and they don't have anything to say to us today in our modern age.

Oh, I think they do. God is speaking to us and talking about the very questions being raised in our newspapers, magazines, online sites, and ethical seminars. Where do we go with all of this? How do I respond to these complex questions as I try to give advice and as I try to pray with someone else?

Just as a court is asked to determine the motive for killing, we must evaluate and determine what our motives are when we are faced with end-of-life decisions.

H. L. Ellison wrote in his Bible study on Exodus:[39]

Life is a gift of God, which cannot be replaced by man if he takes it. ... The prophets extended its meaning to include all that cuts at the roots of life, such as injustice and robbing a man of the means of livelihood. Jesus went further, including every attitude that robbed a man of his self-esteem and that lack of love which meant the withholding of aid when it was most needed (Matthew 5:21–26).

134 · Dr. William B. Coker, Sr.

Abortion

We cannot discuss the application of "You shall not kill" (Exodus 20:13) without looking at the question of abortion. Even though our laws in America state it is legal for a woman to make the decision to seek out an abortion and that she has the right to choose to end the life of her unborn child, is that a morally proper choice?

I listen to the explanations that the fetus is not a person, so having an abortion is not the same as committing murder, and therefore it is not a moral judgment.

One can argue that no one has been able to determine when a person becomes a person, but can we agree that humans conceive humans? We know that when a woman becomes pregnant, she is not going to give birth to a kitten or dog or monkey. And we do know that when a woman becomes pregnant, her offspring is the result of a combination of two sets of human DNA (the mother's and the father's). The DNA says that the child is human, so instead of focusing on the unborn child's humanity, some argue about its personhood.

In 1993, Peter Singer, a bioethics professor at Princeton University, argued that an infant should not be considered a person within the first month of his or her birth.[40] His argument, taken to its logical conclusion is that abortion and infanticide (so long as the infant is less than thirty days old) is not murder. Mr. Singer is not the first person to declare that a child is not a person until it reaches a certain stage of development or awareness, but how do we decide when a person is truly a person?

The sixth commandment does not address the question

of how we identify *persons*; what it does address is the killing of *humans*. When it comes to life, especially human life, we have a responsibility to the sanctity of life. What is the motive for arguing for abortion? Do we say it's acceptable if it means saving the lives of mothers who are at high risk of dying if the pregnancy is continued? Do we believe that is the only concern? Most abortions are done for convenience or used as a cover up. Then that is a different issue all together.

Authority and Right

At the beginning of the chapter I wrote that the sixth word refers to taking a life without right or authority, which raises our final question: is killing ever justified?

That question introduces us to a couple of other thorny issues, doesn't it? It raises the issue of capital punishment. In Genesis 9:5, God tells Noah that He "will require a reckoning for the life of a man."

In the following verse, God clearly states that if one human being kills another, the first one must pay with his life, simply because he is responsible for killing one who bears the image of God. This was not only a word spoken for ancient society. It is a word spoken for contemporary society as well, because God's Word does not change.

What about Romans 13? You can't say the Roman Empire consisted of a bunch of barbarians. Their society was highly developed in marvelous ways. When Paul wrote about the rights of government, he stated that the rulers had a right to bear swords (v. 4) and use them according to God's purpose to avenge wrong. Again, Paul was not speaking to a barbaric society. Scripture states clearly there is a provision for capital punishment. But does that make us feel easy about this procedure? Hardly. We continue to wrestle with this issue.

What about war? Is war ever justified? For hundreds of years men have written about *just* wars. There are times when war is right and just, and when action *must* be taken in order to rescue or preserve life. Others argue against that. They say the answer to the world's ills is not more killing, but an attitude of peace, a posture of non-aggression. They have willingly accepted the fact that they might die at the hands of another because of their strong conviction, but they, themselves, will never take a life. Whether you agree with them or not, you must admire a person who is willing to die rather than take the life of another.

But many of us do not believe this is an adequate solution. The Bible records all kinds of wars, yet we cannot always point to these actions proudly. It is like when we as Christians find ourselves embarrassed regarding the Crusades. We often find that what is supposed to be just, right, and good was anything but that. And now in our own news media when we read about some of the wars that have taken place, we question how we are to deal with what we hear and see.

How do we look at a world that is violent and come up with a solution? It is obvious that none of this violence should be taking place, but we question whether a pacifist posture will ultimately be able to maintain any kind of order and justice in a world like ours. That leaves an uneasy position of saying we are not pacifists, but the support or approval of war is atrocious and ungodly.

I don't know how all this strikes you, but the commandment is there. It is the law of the community God has given to us as His people. And Jesus takes this law another step. In the Sermon on the Mount, Jesus said:

> *You have heard that it was said to those of old, "You shall not murder; and whoever murders will be liable to judgment." But I say to you that everyone who is angry with his brother will be liable to judgment; whoever insults his brother will be liable to the council; and whoever says, "You fool!" will be liable to the hell of fire.*
>
> *—Matthew 5:21–22*

Through my work with the Emmaus Walk, I've discovered a number of women and men whose lives have been damaged and devastated by abusive people in their lives. The abusers may have never committed murder, but they killed. They killed a beautiful part of a person's life, and in some instances, distorted it so completely, that the individual has not fully recovered what had been lost to them.

That's abuse, you say. But what about people who are guilty of character assassination? Gossipers who have destroyed the life of another person by unwarranted words and untrue accusations? According to Christ, all of these things are just as vile as the act of extinguishing a person's physical life.

Pray for Our World

God's sixth word was one of promise and warning. It

was good for the ancient Israelites and it is good for the twenty-first century. How do we return to a place where we honor the lives of those living in society with us? There are many prayers we could pray, beginning with Harry Emerson Fosdick's beautiful hymn, "God of Grace and God of Glory," in which he writes, "Cure Thy children's warring madness."[41]

We can begin by remembering that as members of the body of Christ, we are a covenant people who are called to live in unity, and we should not allow anything in our lives to contribute to the spiritual, physical, or emotional death of another person. With God being our helper, that should be our affirmation of this commandment: "Thou shalt not kill."

WORKBOOK

Chapter Six Questions

Question: What are some practical safety steps that you can take to protect the lives of those in your care and to prevent yourself from accidentally harming the life of another? What professions have extra moral responsibility for the lives of others, and how can those in such professions honor and protect life?

_____

_____

_____

_____

_____

_____

_____

_____

_____

Question: "Maybe the answer to suffering is not what we *get*, but what we have the opportunity to *give*." Describe a person that you know (or know of) who has used their suffering to share Christ and glorify Him. How can a person honor God through illness, disability, or prolonged dying, and what impact can that have on the community around them? How—and what—can severely physically or mentally handicapped people *give* to their caregivers and those who observe their lives?

_____

_____

_____

_____

_____

_____

_____

_____

_____

_____

Question: How can you celebrate life—all life—and help to create and cultivate a culture of life in your home, church, and community? Which lives are looked upon as "less than," and how can you honor them? What resources do you have for those who may consider taking their lives, and how can you foster awareness of the trauma and mental health issues that make a person more vulnerable to committing suicide?

_____

_____

_____

_____

_____

_____

_____

_____

_____

_____

Action: Who has the authority or right to take the life of another? In what context? Research Scripture about the following issues. You may find it helpful to read the positions of prominent church leaders and theologians throughout the centuries. Then come up with your own prayerful, biblically-based positions on the following:

- Killing in self-defense (or to protect another person) by a civilian.

- Killing in self-defense (or to protect others) by a law enforcement officer.

- Killing in war.

- The death penalty.

- End-of-life care.

- Abortion.

Prayer: Lord Jesus, when we look at the evil that has greatly impacted our world—whether through the violence of war or through the violence of neighbor against neighbor, whether violence against the unwanted or undesirable or violence against our children—all of it screams out about the sinfulness of the human heart and the need for redemptive grace. Father, maybe we have taken comfort in the fact that we are not guilty of having unjustifiably taken the life of another person, and yet we have contributed to the character assassination of spreading gossip about another person. Too often we may have been the ones guilty of wrong attitudes toward others. Forgive us, Lord. Help us not to dismiss Your word given to people long ago, for it is as true today as it was then. Make us sensitive to the application of this word with its thorny questions. Help us to be like Christ and to walk in the covenant He has made with us by His blood. We pray in Christ's name. Amen.

Chapter Six Notes

144 · D<small>R</small>. W<small>ILLIAM</small> B. C<small>OKER</small>, S<small>R</small>.

CHAPTER SEVEN

The Seventh Word: Marriage Is a Covenant

You shall not commit adultery.
—*Exodus 20:14*

We now come to the seventh of the words God delivers to Moses and the Israelites: "You shall not commit adultery." Like the previous command, "You shall not murder" (Exodus 20:13), this word is referred to time and again.

While keeping the previous command is not as easy as it sounds, this seventh word extends into areas we might be surprised to think about. Certainly, we can recognize the sexual context in which this occurs, as it seems that the elicit use of sex has been around since sin came into this world. In fact, we would have to say that sexual sin is directly connected with the Fall, because when you go back to Genesis 3 and the story of how Adam and Eve sinned, they instantly became aware of their nakedness and felt shame. God then intervened to provide a covering for them. It introduced a new area to life.

While Adam's and Eve's sin was not sexual in nature, their choice resulted in a fracture of God's ideal for marriage and relationships. Through the centuries, God has had to speak to His people with regard to the boundaries for the proper use of our sex drive.

While what adultery looks like may be debatable in some circles today, it is certainly not debatable in Scripture. God says sex is legitimate and moral within marriage. Period! That means fornication is forbidden, adultery is forbidden, incest is forbidden, homosexuality is forbidden, and prostitution is forbidden. People inside and outside the faith community attempt to say the Bible does not communicate anything about homosexuality being a sin. Every time I hear that claim, it reminds me of the time a woman told me there was nothing against adultery in the Bible. She must have read the Bible with one eye closed. But here it is in Exodus: "Do not commit adultery."

The writer of Ecclesiastes stated, "There is nothing new under the sun" (Ecclesiastes 1:9), and that is also true regarding sexual sin. Again and again, the Israelites had to deal precisely with this problem. They were surrounded by nations that had cult prostitution, and they were drawn into the attractive circles of these cultic groups.

God warned them that, in spite of what others might do, if they are going to live in relationship with Him, they needed to respect the boundary that exists in their covenant relationship, one that does not permit the promiscuous use of sex outside of marriage.

Beyond cultic prostitution, they also engaged in the same sin people still deal with—the matter of the wandering eye. One of the great statements in the book of Job is where he said, "I made a covenant with my eyes not to look lustfully at a young woman" (Job 31:1 NIV). Job sensed the problem was more than an issue of his eyes; it was an issue with his heart. Throughout Scripture, there are others who repeat a similar conviction. The psalmist wrote, "I will set no wicked thing before mine eyes" (Psalm 101:3 KJV).

We can be confident that wickedness includes the problem of sex outside of God's perfect design.

Dangers of Sex

As we go through Scripture, we find the author of Proverbs is explicit when he wrote about the dangers of sex outside of God's established boundaries. He spent a whole chapter on it in a message to his son:

Drink water from your own cistern, flowing water from your own well. Should your springs be scattered abroad, streams of water in the streets? Let them be for yourself alone, and not for strangers with you. Let your fountain be blessed, and rejoice in the wife of your youth, a lovely deer, a graceful doe. Let her breasts fill you at all times with delight; be intoxicated always in her love. Why should you be intoxicated, my son, with a forbidden woman and embrace the bosom of an adulteress? For a man's ways are before the eyes of the LORD, and he ponders all his paths. The iniquities of the wicked ensnare him, and he is held fast in the cords of his sin. He dies for lack of discipline, and because of his great folly he is led astray.

—Proverbs 5:15–23

Whether it is advice of a father for a son, or the priest in the temple, or the prophet who speaks God's word to the people, the message is straight forward. At our own peril we ignore the guidelines God has set in place around sex.

The New Testament addresses some of the same problems. Paul wrote to the people in Corinth that immorality existed within the church, a kind that was not even practiced among the pagans. A man was sleeping with his father's wife and the church was turning a blind eye to it. Paul directly pointed this out and called for the church to take action that resulted in the repentance of the church and the individual (1 Corinthians 5:1–2).

In the sixth chapter of 1 Corinthians, Paul addressed their practice of prostitution (vs. 15–18). He reminded them that they belong fully to Christ and they were "bought with a price" (1 Corinthians 6:19–20). How then could they use their bodies (which are not their own) to commit sin against God? Paul urged them to live in purity and according to the moral code God had set before them.

It is no surprise that the problem in ancient Israel and in New Testament times is still a problem today. We wrestle with sexual sin—not only adults, but also our youth. Ideas abound that all we need to do is *be safe* about it. We defend the practice of passing out condoms to young people who are not yet prepared for the responsibility of a sexual life. We tell them: "It's part of your human nature to do this. Just be safe."

Of course, the question is, are they safe? If we think all we need is a condom or birth control to guide us in our security of safe sex, then there would be no need for abortion, and we would not be pressing for vaccines to protect our children against sexually transmitted diseases. We do not deal honestly by urging our young people to be free in their sexual expression, all the while ignoring the risks that their casual encounters have on their emotional, physical, and spiritual wellbeing.

Furthermore, once we get involved in sexual sin, nature takes its course, and then we want to cover it up. The abortion industry makes its profits from the unwanted consequences of our sin. We may say the grounds for abortion are to save a mother's life and for the cases of rape, but statistics show that since 1973, when abortion became legal, more than 61.6 million babies have been aborted in this country as of 2017.[42] Few incidences have anything to do with rape. A far smaller number than that has anything to do with a mother's life.[43] It's a matter of covering up our mistakes. When we promote and perform this kind of sinful behavior, we need something to take care of unwanted circumstances.

And it doesn't stop there. The advertising industry and the porn industry are making a mint off the obsession we have today with sex. With the rise of cellphones and high-speed internet, we have instant access to the most graphic pictures and videos than anyone has ever had available in history. And the pornographic industry isn't satisfied with adults—a recent study found that children as young as seven are already viewing porn.[44] The results are destroying their ability to form real and healthy relationships, which in turn affects the future wellbeing of our society.

Today's problem is no different than it was at any other time. But God, with great foresight, simply said to the

Israelites, "If you want a safe, secure society—then don't commit sex outside the boundaries of marriage. You need to treat sex the way I created it—with dignity and respect." A simple word.

Deeper Meaning Than Sex

As I said before, this commandment or this word is not primarily about sex. I think there is another issue more deeply involved, one we fail to look at when we only talk about sex and not look at the further significance of this word. The reason I think it's not primarily about sex is two-fold.

First, there is the harsh penalty God gives for this sin. Anyone caught in the act of adultery, the Lord said to the Israelites, was to be put to death (Leviticus 20:10). Because God is absolute in His response to adultery, it becomes clear there is something deeper that He is addressing than the act of sex outside of marriage.

Why does God respond with such severity to something we recognize today as a forgivable sin? There are a couple of ways to look at this. The first is to go back to the fifth word regarding the family and its basic structure, then look at its significance in society; for as the family goes, so goes the nation. If adultery becomes the practice, then you are undermining the basic and most significant institution in human relationships—the family. Think about the lives that have been blighted with this type of liaison between a spouse and someone who is not their marriage partner. Children bear scars of when their family has been torn apart.

Therefore, we can say: Yes, this is an important word because it deals with the family, not only for the preservation of the children, but for society. If we are going to pursue, indiscriminately, this type of lackadaisical and damaging attitude about the use of sex, we will end up destroying the family. By doing so, we affect the nurture of our children, the future generations of our society.

That may seem like a dramatic statement. But I do not see how any Christian today could believe otherwise. One problem we are encountering is young people growing to adulthood with the scars from families that have been ripped apart by this kind of immoral behavior.

Because the Emmaus community is a broad spectrum of churches, it has given me opportunity for interaction and ministry beyond my own congregation. I've been dismayed by how many lives have been affected by damaging family situations. If a survey were taken among people in churches, you would discover that a vast number of people would say their lives have been affected by abuses in this area of sexual sin.

But there's more to it than that. In the previous chapter, regarding the sixth word, I wrote that Jesus explained in the Sermon on the Mount that God's word goes further than the act of murder—it goes down to the thoughts and intents of your heart and mind. If you look at a brother with hatred in your eyes, Jesus said, you are as guilty of murder as if you'd struck him down (Matthew 5:21–22). Immediately after that, He said, "You have heard that it was said, 'You shall not commit adultery.' But I say to you that everyone who looks at a woman with lustful intent has already committed adultery with her in his heart"

(Matthew 5:27–28).

Once again, the word goes deeper than the act. It applies to the attitude and motive. We must look deeper than the outer appearance because God does not look at the outward appearance; He looks at the heart of the person (1 Samuel 16:7).

In the Gospel account, we have the incident of a woman who was caught in the act of adultery. Although we don't know the woman's story, we do know that the religious leaders used this in an attempt to trap Jesus. But instead of His condemning the woman, He drew attention to the accusers. When we look at Jesus' response to this situation, we are given a clue to the deeper meaning of this word from God. After the crowd had left, Jesus looked at the woman and said, "Has no one condemned you?... Neither do I condemn you; go and from now on sin no more" (John 8:10–11).

Significance of the Covenant

The second reason I believe the seventh word is not primarily about sex is because marriage is a reflection of our covenant relationship with God. What exists in a marriage relationship is a covenant between a man and a woman. It is not only the basis of their personal relationship; it is the foundation upon which families are built. But it goes deeper than that. If you want to know what it is like to have a relationship with God, there is no better analogy than to look at the marriage relationship between a husband and wife.

That is what Paul says in Ephesians 5. Husbands are to

love and to dedicate their lives to their wives, and wives are to be submissive (or dedicated) to their husbands. He was talking about a mystery that is Christ and the church (v. 32). Here is the pattern. Here is the example. In this seventh word, you realize what God is saying about marriage—this covenant is to be monogamous. It is to be a wholehearted relationship in which both parties are fully dedicated to each other. It is meant to be a permanent relationship.

The first word God spoke in the Decalogue was: I am the only God. You cannot have any god besides me.

I am convinced that even though polygamist situations are found in the Old Testament, you will discover the relationship God intended between a man and woman in marriage is monogamous. The reason is the pattern, the analogy. I can understand what it is to be yielded to God, because I know what it is to be in a marriage covenant. I want to repeat that another way. When God speaks of our relationship with Him, the infinite with the finite, how are we to grasp that? What do I understand about the very character of that covenant between God and me? He points to marriage.

When you become involved in an adulterous relationship outside of your marriage, you are breaking a covenant. You are striking at what is most significant in your marriage relationship and your covenant with God. What God is addressing in His word to us lies beyond the issue of sex. It is a foundational element about the covenant relationship that a man and woman make with one another, the pattern for our covenant relationship with God.

Betrayal

When you talk to people whose marriages have been affected by adultery, the thing that seems to emerge is the statement, "I feel as if I have been betrayed." Why the sense of betrayal? Because in the marriage covenant, they established a relationship that was to be one of permanence and wholehearted devotion. The couple had made an agreement to separate from others and be devoted only unto each other. They have now betrayed the covenant by the unlawful and unfaithful activities involved.

We are not going to solve the breakdown of the family until we repent of the root cause of its demise. We are living in a society where the absence of commitment to God makes it almost impossible to talk about a covenant like marriage. We can argue about the importance of family and what it does for children, but when it comes to closing the flood gates that have already struck our nation, the place we have to begin as Christians is with ourselves. We cannot change the minds of those people who make no affirmation to God.

God gave the Decalogue to people He had chosen and who responded in their choice of God. For people who make no such commitment of their lives, it is difficult for them even to admit there is anything that should curtail their particular selfish concerns and activities. If they are not committed to God, they ultimately end up being committed to themselves. Thus, in marriage they commit in the sense that it benefits *me*, and what *I* will gain from it.

In his book *Mere Christianity,* C. S. Lewis argued that there ought to be two kinds of marriages. There should be marriage performed in the interest of the state. Then as Christians a second marriage ceremony could be performed before God. Lewis asked: Why should we get people to stand before God and take vows they have no intention of keeping? We make them liars. Lewis further made a rather startling statement: "It is perhaps better that they should live together unmarried than that they should make vows they do not mean to keep."[45]

We as Christians cannot change the attitudes of people in society, but we can address the problem among ourselves. Divorce is a pervasive issue that has likely touched most everyone within the church in some form or fashion. People within the church are also divorcing, and it's a problem.

So, I want to ask questions, not about society, but about Christians. How do we close the flood gates? How do we address the issue of adultery? What do we need to do? I think there are several measures we can take.

Reclaim What Love Is

We need to redefine what love means. A lot of youth growing up in Sunday school have no concept of what love is all about. They associate it with a feeling, yet love is not only pleasure. It involves pleasure, but that is not all. Our youth need to know love is something deeper than feelings. I am convinced that the high divorce rate is largely due to the misconception of thinking marriage is a legal reason for having sex. Just because we feel sexual passion toward another person does not mean that we have a solid foundation for a relationship. While sexual passion is important and has its role, that is not the primary significance of the covenant of marriage.

Scott Peck, in his book *The Road Less Traveled,* has a chapter on love.[46] He states that most of what we say about love has to do with sex. When someone says, "I fell in love," what he means is, "I have sexual passion toward this person." It is an erotic statement, not a statement about love and has more to do with what you can get from another person.

How often has that happened in the backseat of an automobile? Love is something more. As I look at Scripture, I discover that when you deal with passionate love alone, it can quickly turn something good into something quite the opposite.

One of the interesting love stories you find in the Old Testament is in 2 Samuel 13. It is the story about Amnon, David's son, and his half-sister Tamar. She must have been a beautiful young lady, because Amnon looked at her and became desirous of having her. The passage relates that when he looked at her, he loved her so much he made himself ill. He devised a plan to take advantage of her. He pretended being sick one day, knowing that someone would bring him his lunch. So, he requested that Tamar serve him. They would be alone; the stage would be set.

The story goes that Tamar brought Amnon his lunch, and as she drew near, he grabbed her, pulled her into his bed and raped her. End of story? Not by a longshot. Absalom, his brother, took vengeance. But far worse than the feud that erupted is what Scripture says after Amnon got what he wanted: "...the hatred with which he hated her was greater than the love with which he had loved her" (2

Samuel 13:15).

That story has been repeated over and over throughout history. This is why every teenage girl, young unmarried ladies, and married partners need to understand that if the attraction is merely sexual passion, it often turns into something far different. That is why a girl who has been talked into giving up her virginity often finds that the guy loses respect for her and wants nothing more to do with her. That which was supposed to be beautiful, when isolated, becomes the most perverse and vile act that affects lives.

What do we mean by true love, then? Real love is a lifelong *choice* based on mutual respect and mutual appreciation. It's not simply an attraction. For a long time, when I did pre-marital counseling, I would remind young people there are several Greek words for the idea of love. The one used most is *agape* with a minimum of emotion and a maximum of evaluation. The key idea is respect. When respect is missing, we find that marriage is based upon what cannot long sustain it. Love is a choice based on mutual respect and appreciation, which develops into a desire to be together and become one in the biblical sense of the term. All these aspects work together in their proper order.

Redefine Marriage

Not only do we have to redefine love, we must also redefine marriage. What does marriage mean? In our day it is a civil contract made before the state. As a pastor performing a wedding, I am legally bound to say: "By the authority vested in me by the state of Indiana, I pronounce you husband and wife."

That is my responsibility. The state accepts the fact that I have performed the wedding and that both parties are in agreement that they have entered into a binding contract. A civil covenant is necessary for the state and holds the couple responsible for their marriage and the children born into that marriage. The state has a vested interest in a couple's vows to each other. But what we as believers are declaring in the ceremony goes deeper than that. It goes to the relationship, the covenant, between a man and a woman.

So, if we redefine marriage and rediscover what marriage is all about in the churches of America, Christians would begin speaking and teaching that marriage for us is not a civil contract or a business deal. The problem with a business deal is you are in it until a better one comes along. But marriage is more. It is a covenant made in the presence of Almighty God, a covenant made according to the dictates of our Sovereign God to whom we belong and serve.

There are several aspects a marriage covenant covers:

- Covenant establishes the privileges and responsibilities of marriage, and we need to understand those terms.

- A marriage covenant fulfills the purpose of two becoming one as God described in the book of Genesis and referenced in Ephesians 5 and other places. There is a unitary purpose for marriage. In male and female, you have in each an incompleteness that finds wholeness only as the two become one.

• Marriage provides the social structure into which we can bring children. Not only are we responsible for procreation of children in our image but nurturing those children so they can grow in stature and in the knowledge of God. It's our responsibility that they grow in understanding, knowledge, and wisdom.

• What marriage before God does is make public the fact of sex. That does not mean sex is done publicly; it means that the sexual relationship between the husband and wife becomes common knowledge to everyone. With a husband and wife, sex is part of their relationship, the marriage union, including its vows and its practice. A marriage covenant made before God publicly acknowledges and establishes responsibility for this aspect of their relationship.

Make a Stand

The problem with premarital sex is that it wants to exploit the pleasure without accepting the responsibility. It wants to exploit the physical pleasure without the oneness of persons. That is why the church needs to continue to stand against premarital sex. Not only is it not right; it's not good.

You ask why I would make that statement for the benefit of the church. It's because someone years ago told me he belonged to a Sunday school class of young, single adults, and in their discussion, they were amazed that pre-marital sex was not acceptable.

When the Bible describes adultery, it does speak about physical adultery, but the word frequently occurs in a spiritual context as well.

> *You adulterous people! Do you not know that friendship with the world is enmity with God? Therefore whoever wishes to be a friend of the world makes himself an enemy of God.*
> —*James 4:4*

If you are going to have a relationship with the world, there will be hostility between you and God; therefore, do not commit adultery. There you find the significance of this seventh word. Sexual sin will wreck families and destroy society. Not only that, it will break down the analog—the pattern—by which you can understand what God and humanity have established between them.

The good word is that God forgives adultery, as Jesus forgave the woman brought before Him. That is what the story of Jesus is all about in John 8. God not only forgives physical adultery, but also spiritual adultery, of which we all are guilty. The good news here is that with God there is forgiveness and for that we say, thank God.

WORKBOOK

Chapter Seven Questions

Question: What are your greatest sexual temptations or stumbling blocks? What does the Bible have to say about these specifics that tempt or ensnare you, and how would obeying God's plan allow you to experience the love, freedom, and purpose He has for your sexuality?

_____

_____

_____

_____

_____

_____

_____

_____

Question: What are some of the thoughts, habits, and associations that can lead to adultery? What heart issues have already taken place before an affair begins? How can a proper understanding of the marriage covenant (and of your covenant relationship with God) help to prevent the attitudes that lead to adultery?

_____

_____

_____

_____

_____

_____

_____

_____

_____

_____

_____

Question: Give examples of sexual sin in both the Old and New Testament. What consequences followed? How did God offer forgiveness and restoration to the sinning individual? How does He forgive our spiritual adultery?

_____

_____

_____

_____

_____

_____

_____

_____

_____

_____

_____

_____

_____

Action: Interview two or three Christian couples who have been happily married for 40–50 years or more. What practical steps did they take to remain faithful to each other, or if there was betrayal, how did they work through it to restore the relationship? How would they define love and the purpose of marriage? What advice would they give to single people looking for a spouse or to a young couple in their first years of marriage?

Prayer: Father, in what seems to be a clear and simple word, You have brought us face to face with a problem that's becoming more acceptable in our society. We have championed the idea that sex is a matter between consenting adults. We live in a sex-saturated society, and even our children know too much too young. Speak to those of us, Father, who are guilty of lust in the heart. We are grateful that You provide forgiveness. If any of us are guilty of sexual sin, may we make our confession and be assured of Christ's sacrifice for our redemption. May our churches restore the meanings of love and the marriage covenant. Forgive us also of any spiritual adultery and restore us as individuals in covenant relationship with You, so that we may redeem our world. We pray in Christ's name. Amen.

Chapter Seven Notes

CHAPTER EIGHT

The Eighth Word:
It All Belongs to God

You shall not steal.

—Exodus 20:15

The eighth word is simply, "Do not steal." It seems like a simple word, but I guarantee that it is fraught with a great deal more difficulty for understanding and applying it to our lives than we may think. When God spoke this word, He was letting us know that He is concerned not only with maintaining His relationship with His people and our relationship with Him; He is also concerned with the integrity of the people who are known by His name. We are reminded in Ezekiel 36:16–21 that God's people could profane the name of God both in terms of their condition and conduct.

Whether we look at God's words to Israel as commands or words of endearment, one fact remains: these words recorded in the book of Exodus address how God wants His people to live.

As with God's previous words, God's instruction not to steal is not a threatening, dire command so much as it is a guideline to establish a society where integrity can be maintained. In the commandment about honoring our parents, we are called to maintain integrity in the relationship between parents and children. We should not kill because we want to maintain the integrity of every individual. Every person has been created in the image of God and to be respected for that reason. In the seventh command, we honor marriage, the sacred union between a husband and wife. We are people of integrity, and thus we are faithful to the covenant established between us.

Now in this eighth word, God says we are to maintain integrity in how we view and handle what we call "goods" or "possessions." Everything we have stems from God's provision for us, whether it be food, clothing, homes, or the newest gadget. These things are all meant to be good, but when a person violates this God-given word, we introduce into society a destructive force that threatens the integrity (strength or soundness) of the community. Stealing is built on the concept of deceit. Deceit gives birth to distrust, followed by disaffection. Thus, one action by one individual affects all of society in ways that go far beyond the loss of personal property.

When I last visited New Orleans, I went to the neighborhood where I had lived while growing up. I remember delivering newspapers in a delightful community filled with friendly people, but upon my return I saw bars on all the windows. Block after block reminded me that life in the big city is now one of distrust. We put bars on our windows and locks on our doors because we know people cannot be trusted.

The same is true of communication. Many people now screen their calls when they don't recognize the number that appears on the Caller ID. For all we know, the person on the other end is a scammer looking to obtain personal information he can use to steal our identity. A history of theft, whether we've personally experienced it or only heard of others' experiences, not only creates a feeling of distrust, but a break between individuals. The end result is disaffection toward others in society.

So, when God said, "Do not steal," He was not simply giving us a rule for eternal life. He was giving us a practical boundary to protect the unity of our society and to protect ourselves. The primary motivator of theft is greed, one of the seven deadly sins called avarice. Greed is the passion to possess something that an individual has become obsessed with. When greed rules our hearts, it's a grinding insensitivity to other people. We do not care how our actions affect those around us. We are only concerned with our consuming need to have that object that has taken top place in our lives. In essence, it becomes the idol we worship and the god we will do anything to serve.

Boundaries

For our protection, God knew we needed boundaries. This idea of boundaries is present everywhere, especially in the sports world. In a football game, you see markings on the field. You can only play the game within those boundaries. If you get outside them, the game is halted, and you are penalized for disrupting the flow of the game. However, if you play within the rules, you get to enjoy the fun and entertainment of the game.

God's boundaries for living affect society and individuals. When we live within His framework, life is pleasant. When we don't, there are consequences. We often quote Jeremiah 29:11 when life is difficult: to remind us that God's plans are not for evil, but for good. Do we remember that at the time Jeremiah wrote this letter, most of the people of Israel were living in exile because they had turned their back on the covenant they'd made with God and with each other? Do we remember that their entire society had broken down as a result of their actions?

When God spoke to His people through Jeremiah, He reminded them that this season of discipline was meant to draw them back to Him and that He would fulfill His promise to restore them (Jeremiah 35:15).

In the same way today, God tells us to live inside the boundaries He's given us so that we can discover the good He has created for us. But if we choose to go outside of His boundaries, we are going to introduce problems into society that destroy it, and it will destroy us in the process. "Do not steal" is every bit a boundary marker as "Do not murder" and "Do not commit adultery." So, what does God mean by "stealing"?

Possession Is Limited

The readings I have been doing on this subject say that we cannot understand the act of theft until we understand the biblical concept for property. When we think of property, we think something simple, such as what I own or what I possess. If somebody asks me about my property, I can begin to enumerate my possessions. But, of course, the question immediately is, do I really possess them? Or do I just use them? Do I own something in an absolute sense? Or is the ownership I claim limited?

The simple answer is: if I died today, I would no longer have claim to any of my possessions. They would pass along to someone else. Therefore, I own nothing in an absolute, permanent sense. I can enjoy the use of my things, but I only possess them in a limited way.

When I think about possessions this way, I realize that I need to occupy myself with something other than accumulating more things. I want something deeper and more lasting. When I listen to God's word, I hear Him saying something else about property.

With capitalism being a predominate way of life in our country, private ownership is of great importance to us. We don't just possess those things, we are defined by them, which leads to two dangerous obstacles in our walk with the Lord: first, I forget who I am; and second, I forget who really owns my stuff.

The psalmist told us, "The earth is the LORD's and the fullness thereof, the world and those who dwell therein, for he has founded it upon the seas and established it upon the rivers" (Psalm 24:1–2). Putting it into our language: The earth is the Lord's, and everything in it belongs to Him. This knowledge should not only affect how we look at the world, but how we listen to the words God speaks to us. Nothing belongs to any of us. No amount of earthly treasure that we accumulate is going to make us anything other than what we already are: part of God's creation.

Jesus certainly underscored that fact in the stories He told. The parable of the talents (Matthew 25:14–30) was about one man who was given ten talents, another given five talents, and a third man given one talent. These talents were given, not owned, with the intent to develop them. We also recognize that not everyone is given equally, because some will receive ten, some will receive five, and some will receive one. What's important, Jesus tells us, is not how much each has received, but how we use what God has entrusted to us. What we possess, even in a capitalist society, is not ours.

Not a Possession but a Trust

Both the Old and New Testaments underscore that what I have is loaned to me. It is a trust. I have something I can use for a period, but ultimately it reverts to the one who created it and whose it is. I am concerned, not with acquiring more and more, but with what I do with what I have. The focus begins to shift from possessing to using. It is also not using more and more. It is how I use what I have been given, what God has entrusted to me.

My great desire now is not to be a person of wealth, but a person of stewardship. I am in a trust relationship with God. He expects me to use things in a way that brings honor and glory to Him. The key word for me is *faithfulness*.

How have I used what has been entrusted to me? Jesus never condemned the man for having only one talent. His word against this man was that he did not use what he had.

It's important for us to understand that the name of the game is not "he who gets the most toys wins." The main issue is: How do we use what is committed to us as a trust?

If it is a trust, that means we are held accountable for the use of what we have. You notice in Jesus' parable, the owner never set a standard for wanting more from the men who received ten or five talents. He only wanted them to use what had been given.

We often beg off doing certain things at times because we think, "I am not a person of great wealth, nor a person of great talent." In the process, we have excused ourselves from the stewardship of life. Whatever we have is a trust and, as stewards, we are accountable to God to use all that He has given us. We will be held accountable to a holy God; we will be held accountable to the stewardship God has entrusted to us.

God is not interested in how much you have. He is interested in what you do with what you have. It is a trust He has given to you. The focus is not on possessing, but on using.

What Is Stealing?

When it comes to the boundaries God sets, we would prefer to define those terms in a rather broad way. Ambiguity breeds comfort. We want to make life comfortable for ourselves. But there is great danger when we attempt to paint God's words with broad strokes. There's the danger of destroying social conscience. In America, it is already fairly low. What disqualifies someone for a job position? What is defined as wrong? Is our social conscience so hardened that we can't distinguish between right and wrong?

When I served as academic dean of a college, it was my responsibility to nominate students from our school who qualified for Who's Who Among Students in American Colleges and Universities. They had set standards. For example, a senior student had to have a certain grade point average (GPA) and be involved in campus life. One young man came very close to being included in Who's Who. The only problem was his GPA was not high enough. He had fouled up in his first year of college but made excellent grades the following three years. When he approached me about his grades, he pointed out their excellence. I stated that his grades from three years were not the question. It was his total accumulative GPA that fell short of the mark.

It would have been easy for me to make an exception for him, because he was a good student and a decent young man. But to accommodate him, I would have to declare that the rules set for the award were no longer valid. Had I nominated the student and he'd won the award, it would have robbed other students who truly deserved to be recognized.

Do we define stealing in such a broad way that we don't know what it is? Not only is our social conscience hardened, but is our personal ethic also sliding? What we used to find wrong, we now accept as part of society. I define stealing as *taking something by unjust means that belongs rightfully to someone else*, no matter what the monetary value. I'm including the theft of one's name.

Robbing persons of their good name through gossip—

saying something we cannot verify, and that may or may not be true—is stealing. Shakespeare said it best in *Othello*: "Who steals my purse steals trash ... but he that filches from me my good name robs me of that which not enriches him, and makes me poor indeed."[47]

Some parents have stolen life from their children through verbal and physical abuse, and sometimes sexual abuse. That child is crippled for the rest of his or her life.

Robbery is obvious if someone points a gun at you and asks for your money or if your house has been burglarized. But what about some other areas?

What about corporate theft? I've heard about businesses buying up smaller businesses and, in the process, transferring debt in order to show the business is debt free, and then they sell it for a huge profit. If they accumulate enough debt to the business that is left, they can declare bankruptcy. Is this shrewd business or stealing? While it may be shrewd in the eyes of the world, it could be called stealing. They have stolen money that should not have been theirs.

People have come against the tobacco industry for the damage done to individual lives. I am waiting for the day when the same tactics will be brought against the alcohol industry. Who wants to argue that alcohol has not had an adverse effect on American society?

Gambling is another form of legalized theft. The whole setup on gambling is not so the person who gambles gets a good chance at winning. It is built instead on profits. A casino moves into an area and says they guarantee to provide jobs and have profits that will pay large taxes. How are they going to do that if it is a fair shake?

Where I grew up in New Orleans, we called the slot machines "one-armed bandits." They were in every service station. The whole defense of the gambling industry is to give people an opportunity for a better life. I want to suggest that *fewer* people have a better life, and more who live at a lower level of ability. People believe they will never see large amounts of money unless they win the lottery. But the truth is: if young people would begin early to put small amounts a month into savings, by the time they retire, they would have what they need.

That practice means we must discipline ourselves. It means we curtail our possessing and getting. But if there is an easy way to get it, we are all for it. What we have engendered in this country is a wrong attitude, one that is ultimately destructive.

There is also the issue of wages and work. Some practices have been done in the name of profit that may be shrewd, but they are wrong. Companies in this country are closing their factories so they can move them to other countries to produce the products in order to save money. I am disturbed when jobs are being taken away from Americans so products can be made cheaper in other countries, and then sold at the same price or higher for the sake of profit. Is there a question of thievery at this point? We may legalize it and say it's alright, but is it?

Let's ask some questions closer to home. I believe that employers have a moral responsibility for the treatment of their workers (1 Timothy 5:18). Is it right for a woman to receive lower wages than a man would be paid for the same job? Are we taking advantage of people in order to make a sale? Have we taken an opportunity from a co-worker or neighbor that rightfully should be theirs?

I also affirm that workers have a moral responsibility to their employers in regard to their work ethic (Colossians 3:23–24). When we come to our work, we want the benefits, but are we willing to give the excellence that it demands of us? Do we justify our actions by saying it's not a big deal?

Either we address these practices in our society, or they eventually prove to be counter-productive. Ultimately, they destroy us as a people. They deaden our social conscience, and they make us less aware of our moral responsibility toward one another. When we forget this, everybody suffers as a result. As Americans, we have sold our souls for profits. But God has another word for it: the word is *stealing*.

When we define the idea of stealing to the typical, like the theft of money or precious valuables, we are able to soothe our consciences when we stray into gray areas that can cause harm to our integrity as individuals and as a society. As God's people, we need to recognize that there is a great danger with this attitude. When we justify our actions by saying they're not *that* bad, our conscience becomes seared, and it becomes harder and harder to recognize the difference between right and wrong. Once we reach that point, what is left? Where do we go from there?

Stealing Is Not Only About Money

Finally, I want us to look at the most important, the most commonly ignored case of theft. We find it in the book of Malachi. "Will man rob God? Yet you are robbing me. But you say, 'How have we robbed you?' In your tithes and contributions" (Malachi 3:8).

You mean the Bible teaches that if I do not take a tenth of what I possess to recognize God's ownership of everything, then I am robbing Him? That is God's word. That is what He says. I am robbing Him of my tithes and offerings.

I have learned through the years that wherever my checkbook leads me, I will discover my god at the end of that path. I know that unless I honor God with what He has entrusted to me, then I will not honor Him in the other areas of my life. As I said before, theft is stronger and more inclusive than being about money and valuables; it also includes our service to God.

How many of us are robbing God of our time? When the church bulletin asks for nursery team workers and classroom teachers, and we say we don't have the time to volunteer for one more thing, are we robbing God by our lack of response?

In our churches, we must have a renewing of the Holy Spirit in our lives and come to a time of revival. Because unless we do that and begin to sense there is more than walking in the door, singing songs, and hearing a word from the pastor, we are robbing God of our service. We cannot be satisfied with being saved and going to heaven one day. There is more. Our world desperately needs the gospel of Jesus Christ. We give of ourselves so that others may hear. We serve others so that we may show the love of Christ to a hurting world. That is our privilege in building the kingdom of God.

I don't want to live in a society where theft is rationalized away and where people close their eyes to what's right and wrong. I want to live in a world where people recognize what is good, what is right, and live with integrity as a result. I want to live in a church where we also say we have a responsibility and debt to our God. What I do, I do not because it pays. I do it for God's sake; I do it for the kingdom of God.

My faithfulness is not only to my society. My faithfulness is to my God whom I serve and to whom I ultimately belong—as does everything I think I possess right now.

Palms Down

I heard a pastor who was once a missionary in India. He said when the Indian Christians talk about their commitment to God, they describe it as *palms down*. We can't hang on to anything when our palms are turned down. That is one of the most beautiful descriptions I have ever heard of what my commitment to God needs to be. Palms down.

God made us. He owns us and everything in the world. How foolish it would be for us to have closed hands—or hands that grasp for things that are not ours—when we have a God who is already and always open-handed in His blessings to us. I can testify to God's generosity to me, and if you're honest, you can do the same.

WORKBOOK

Chapter Eight Questions

Question: List some of the industries that exist because of various types of theft and the resulting mistrust in society. What would a society look like where a person's word could be believed and where property, identity, or intellectual theft are rare? How would the financial and social landscape of the nation and individuals be significantly different? How would the workplace be different if employers and employees were both committed to obeying God's word regarding stealing?

_____

_____

_____

_____

_____

_____

_____

_____

_____

_____

_____

_____

Question: Do you think of your possessions as your own or as a trust from God? What actions and attitudes will accompany each of these mindsets? How will becoming a wise steward of what God has entrusted to you help you avoid theft in all of its various forms? Have you ever robbed God in time or money?

_____

_____

_____

_____

_____

_____

_____

_____

_____

_____

_____

Question: How does financial management relate to the idea of not stealing? How do both debt and charging interest create temptations to steal? How can Christians manage their finances in a way that honors God and avoids any form of theft?

_____

_____

_____

_____

_____

_____

_____

_____

_____

_____

Action: Memorize Ephesians 4:28. What honest work has God given you to do? What do you have to share with those in need? Write down three ways you can develop a diligent, hardworking attitude and three ways you can develop a generous, giving spirit. Choose one of each to begin focusing on in the weeks ahead.

Prayer: Lord Jesus, as Your followers, we look at this commandment not to steal and hear something that addresses every one of us. We know there's the temptation to have our conscience hardened. We ask that Your Holy Spirit help us to respond with honesty to Your call and the boundaries set for us. We are grateful that You have loved us abundantly and given to us in such great measure, asking only that we respect the integrity of goods belonging to others and the privilege we have to give of our own possessions. Most of all, may we strive never to rob You by withholding our offerings of money, time, or service. We pray in Your name and for Your glory. Amen.

Chapter Eight Notes

CHAPTER NINE

The Ninth Word:
Speak Truth

You shall not bear false witness against your neighbor.
—Exodus 20:16

We look now at the ninth of the ten words God spoke to His people. The principle itself does not need much elaboration, but when we stop to think about what God is saying, it broadens into much more than these few words. The ninth word tells us not to bear false witness against our neighbor.

As we read the ten words, we discover a maintenance program. They were not the means of redemption. God rescued His people out of the land of bondage and brought them into freedom. God gave them His covenant: "All the people answered together and said, 'All that the LORD has spoken we will do'" (Exodus 19:8).

It's important to remember that when God spoke these words, He wasn't establishing rules for us to follow in order to be saved. He had already redeemed Israel when He rescued them out of Egypt, and He redeemed us when Christ died on the cross. These words, these guidelines, were designed as a framework to maintain a whole and healthy society whose foundation was established in a committed relationship with God.

In this book, we have focused on social relationships—how we are to maintain ourselves—not only as a people of God, but with one another. Each aspect of society is addressed in this maintenance program. The fifth commandment speaks to the maintenance plan for the family. "Honor your father and mother." In the sixth word, there's a maintenance plan regarding human life. "Do not kill; do not take the life of a person unjustly." Then in the seventh commandment, there was the word for the maintenance of marriage, that most intricate and intimate of human relationships. In the eighth word, we noticed the maintenance of proper respect for the goods of one another.

Now we come to God's word for the maintenance of justice and truth. It is at the heart of the relationships of people. No nation survives long that does not keep a strict eye on the maintenance of justice.

Once, while visiting a courthouse, I spotted a plaque that said, "The price of liberty is eternal vigilance."[48] Liberty honors truth. Truth is of such importance that, in his essay on prudence, Ralph Waldo Emerson wrote: "Every violation of truth is not only a sort of suicide in the liar, but is a stab at the health of human society."[49]

God made it clear from the very beginning that He is concerned with justice and truth. He repeatedly stated that this matter of justice and truth is essential if people are going to live together, if they are to maintain the moral integrity of both individual and society. And this is why He warned us not to "bear false witness against our neighbor."

To Answer

There are a couple of details I want to point out about this word from the Hebrew text. When it was written down, specific Hebrew concepts and words were chosen. For example, we translate the verb as "do not bear" false witness. The Hebrew word *ānâ* means "to answer,"[50] so if you were to translate this ninth word literally, it would say: Do not answer a false witness against your neighbor. In a broader translation, that involves the idea of a testimony.

Why the word *answer*? It is because the word indicates a response to people or situations. This definition is helpful to me. How do I respond to a given situation? The word is talking about how people relate to other people and the social circumstances in which they find themselves.

Empty Words

Second, there is a difference between the passages in Exodus and Deuteronomy at this point. In Exodus it says, "You will not bear a false witness." In the Hebrew, this refers to that which is untrue. We translate it as "false." If a statement is not in agreement with reality, then it is false. You should not bear such a witness or respond to a person in a false manner.

Deuteronomy 5:20 also says, "You shall not give false testimony against your neighbor" (NIV), but what's interesting is the use of the Hebrew word *shaw*, which means "vanity," for the phrase "give false testimony."[51] The concept here is that you should not respond to your neighbor in any kind of vain or worthless or empty way. You must speak the truth, and the truth always relates to something that is worthy, meaningful, and has significance. It has reality because it is true.

When we look at these words, we also see it is clearly talking about the judicial process. When people live together, life does not always work out in harmony. God said there is a right way and a wrong way to reconcile differences. How you handle those differences makes all the difference in society.

The same thing is true in marriage. The idea that when two people come together there will be instantaneous harmony is wishful thinking. We know we differ among ourselves. In marriage, what's vital is how we respond to the difference that exists.

How do I respond to the person to whom I am married when I don't agree with what's been said? How do I respond to the situation that has been created by my spouse? As a husband, I am in relationship and covenant with my wife, as we both are with God. The question is how do I respond to situations when there is a difference in opinion or approach?

The word of God tells me that I am to respond in honesty and truthfulness. I am not to speak falsely or speak in any way that is untrue to reality or the facts. I am not to

WORDS OF ENDEARMENT · 189

respond in any kind of empty way. I am to speak the truth. That is true in matters of justice, and we depend on that.

One of my favorite passages is found in Isaiah 59, where the prophet is dealing with the moral state of the nation. Isaiah is speaking about the terrible acts that have happened in Israel, resulting in their social decline and exile. Because they have not acted honestly with one another, God's judgment is against them and His wrath is descending upon them. The fourth verse applies appropriately to what is said in this ninth word:

> No one enters suit justly; no one goes to law honestly; they rely on **empty pleas** [shaw], they **speak lies**, they conceive mischief and give birth to iniquity.
>
> Therefore justice is far from us, and righteousness does not overtake us; we hope for light, and behold, darkness, and for brightness, but we walk in gloom. We grope for the wall like the blind; we grope like those who have no eyes; we stumble at noon as in the twilight, among those in full vigor we are like dead men.
>
> —*Isaiah 59:4, 9–10* (emphasis added)

That is the problem when justice needs to be served, and when men forget what is true and pursue what is false. The word God gives in Exodus 20:16 is an appropriate word, not only for the nation of Israel, but for us today, because it is vital to life, to our relationships, and to human society. I am impressed by all the places in Scripture where this courtroom concept comes to bear. God says that in the judicial process, what must prevail is truthfulness. The administration of justice is of great concern to

God, as we see in Deuteronomy 19 when He established the strict punishment for those who purposely testify falsely against someone:

> If a malicious witness arises to accuse a person of wrongdoing, then both parties to the dispute shall appear before the LORD, before the priests and the judges who are in office in those days. The judges shall inquire diligently, and if the witness is a false witness and has accused his brother falsely, then you shall do to him as he had meant to do to his brother. So you shall purge the evil from your midst.
> —*Deuteronomy 19:16–19*

What's interesting is where they go to appear for dealing with this witness. They stand "before the LORD" because the integrity of witness in judicial process is not only between two individuals, it includes our relationship to God.

Law and Judicial Process

We find in this ninth word a principle about judicial process—about responsibility and the fact that we are called upon to render true judgment. We are responsible for speaking truth, because justice in the nation is not simply the concern of those in places of leadership; it is a concern for all people. If justice does not prevail, then the nation will not only experience destruction from the corrosive influences of evil—which is what Scripture says— but also because without truth and justice, society cannot long endure.

The idea that it doesn't make much of a difference

when a person lies under oath is without justification, for the issue is not only about a particular case, but what is *necessary* for the maintenance of justice, righteousness, and truth in a nation. It does not make any difference how significant a case may or may not be; what is more important than anything else is that the truth be spoken.

I do not profess to understand everything that's to be known about the law, but it seems there is something in our society that's key to this idea of biblical justice. In every situation where a social conflict must be solved through judicial process, the commitment of everyone concerned should be that justice prevails and the truth is established.

When you hear or read the news, it seems the responsibility of the prosecutor is to convict an individual, and the responsibility of the defense attorney is to get the accused off at whatever price. How irresponsible that is! The responsibility of the prosecutor and of the defense attorney is one and the same. It is justice and truth. That is what we are after. Anything other than that strikes a blow at the heart of society itself.

When you read these instances where lawyers are saying, "It is my job as the attorney of the defendant to get him off in whatever way I can," that is not right. The job is for the good of society, which says justice *must* prevail. It goes back to this word God spoke to the people, and this is not inconsequential. When you think of all God could have said—as He set boundaries for the nation of Israel—the fact that He chose to say what He did tells us that every one of these words is *crucial*. They are vital to the substance of society; they are vital to the maintenance of morality in human relationships.

Whether we live in the twenty-first century or before the time of Christ, vital to human relationship is the triumph of truth. When we sacrifice truth, it is "a stab at the health of human society."[52] We depend on it. This is why it is vital for us to see what God wants of us—to be a people of truth and honesty, a people after His own heart.

In a court of law, it is necessary for truth to triumph. And if a prosecutor keeps certain evidence from coming to the floor because it weakens his case, to that extent he has compromised the truth and dealt a blow to justice in America. To whatever extent a defense attorney seeks to get his client off at whatever price, he has struck a blow at our liberty. He has struck a blow against the justice system. It's that simple.

The Tongue

The word God gave to Israel, however, goes further than the judicial process. Broader terms need to rest upon our hearts. For example, look at the letter James wrote to the early church. In the third chapter, he devoted a paragraph on the devastation of the tongue.

How great a forest is set ablaze by such a small fire! And the tongue is a fire, a world of unrighteousness. The tongue is set among our members, staining the whole body, setting on fire the entire course of life, and set on fire by hell. For every kind of beast and bird, of reptile and sea creature, can be tamed and has been tamed by mankind, but no human being can tame the tongue. It is a restless evil, full of deadly poison. With it we bless our Lord and Father, and with it we

curse people who are made in the likeness of God. From the
same mouth come blessing and cursing. My brothers, these
things ought not to be so.

—James 3:5b–10

The tongue, James said, is like a terrible fire; left un-
guarded, it is enough to destroy society. In looking at
bearing false witness, I have to say that God's word goes
beyond a court of law. It goes to any instance where we
speak something other than what's true. When we do, we
have compromised God's maintenance plan, and we have
crossed the boundary God has set for His people.

In Proverbs we find this word: "A man who bears false
witness against his neighbor is like a war club, or a sword,
or a sharp arrow" (Proverbs 25:18). That's exactly what
James said in his letter. That is exactly what the "Wisdom
of Solomon" in the Apocrypha goes to great length to establish. Words are not idle things; they are instruments
that strike deadly blows at times to the life of another individual. Words are powerful. We find in Scripture the
necessity of being careful that we speak the truth.

There is an interesting detail in Hebrew that I believe
bears a lot of thought. The Hebrew word for *word* is
dabâr, which translates into "a thing."[53] The word for
speak is *dabar*.[54]

If you were going to say, "I don't speak Hebrew," you
would use the word *dabar*. But if you say a *word* in Hebrew, that is *dabâr*. The word for *word*, even in modern
Hebrew, means "a thing." So, if you were saying to someone in modern Hebrew, "Well, it is nothing," you would
use *andabâr*—that is, "It is not a word; it is nothing."

In studying Hebrew in the Old Testament, I discovered there was no distinction between the idea of a *word* and a *thing* in the sense that a word spoken has as much objective reality as a thing or an object.

Just as God created something the moment He spoke during the days of creation, you create something the minute you say something. At whatever point you have uttered a word, whether it is a word of truth or a falsehood, you have brought something into existence that never ceases to be, even though you may repent of it. It is a reality you have created. It is there. When you speak an untruth against another individual, you have brought something into existence. No matter how many apologies you may make to the other individual, what you have created is real. It does not go away. It is a *thing*.

When Scripture talks about the tongue and the use of a word, it does so in solemn terms, because God wants us to realize what we say is absolutely essential to the kind of society in which we live and the kind of life we live. Individually and corporately, words are important.

Unjust Accusations

The ninth word is that we should not bear false witness, that we should not respond to another person falsely, and that we should not make unjust accusations. Why is there such a readiness to believe a word spoken, especially a negative word? Why does it seem to be, even among church people, that we hang onto a juicy morsel? Why are we so ready to believe the worst about someone else?

Most of us could probably think of someone we don't

like. It's not that there is hostility between us, but we prefer to stay away from that person. We don't like their personality or their way of dealing with issues. So, if we have a choice, we simply separate ourselves from that person. Then when a negative word is spoken about that person's character, we are ready to accept it, whether it's true or not.

In some instances, if I dislike a person, it is easy for me to believe the negative. In our multi-ethnic culture, it is easy for us to build walls between ourselves and to believe what is not true about those who come from a different socio-economic background from us. We have pre-judged that person. We do it not only among nationalities, but among Christian denominations. We have a readiness to believe that which is wrong about someone else. We are predisposed not to believe the truth, but to believe what's damaging. There's a word for this mental predisposition: *prejudice.*

Justice is not only a matter of what I speak, but a matter of what I am ready and willing to believe and accept. For the good of society, I need to realize I cannot allow jealousy, prejudice, or personal dislike to influence what I accept as the truth. I am responsible for what I choose to believe about another person.

One of the problems inside the church—as much outside the church—is the gossip line. "Have you heard about John?" We share something we cannot verify, something that may not be true. Why are we prone to do that? Is it because we want to be in the center of the conversation? If I have a nice juicy story to tell, everybody listens. For a moment, I am at the center of attention.

Is there such a sense of selfishness and self-serving in my life that leads me to push down another in order to prop myself up? Even if I have first-hand knowledge of what I'm saying, I am bringing harm to the person I'm speaking about and to the person I'm speaking to, who will then likely go on and share this second-hand information with others.

I know of one situation where someone had spoken a false word about a pastor friend who had gone through a divorce. It was not pleasant. The pastor had not wanted to end his marriage, nor could he keep it from happening. I knew the hurt he went through. The hurt was compounded when, down the road, someone passed the word around that the pastor had remarried, and he had been involved with that woman before his first wife divorced him.

There was not a word of truth to the story, but it was being whispered in a church group. Those who spoke it and those who believed it participated in the slander. The reputation of two of God's children was tarnished.

When you repeat a falsehood, you become a participant. When you say something you don't know if it's true, and others accept it, you promote a false accusation against someone. Likewise, when you share something that is true about someone else, whether it's with malicious intent or not, you are responsible for the life those words take on.

Embellishing Truth

Truth is based on fact. Whenever we exaggerate something that is otherwise correct, we taint the truth. I've

listened to stories told by teachers and pastors, and I wondered: Is this an embellishment, trying to make the gospel
look more appealing to those outside of the faith?

I heard a preacher say once that while driving he noticed his gas tank was empty. He said, "O God, I need gas
for my tank," and he watched as the gas needle went from
empty to full. I am a skeptic when I hear stories like this.
Is God able to do that? He absolutely can do anything He
wants to do. That is why I am not troubled about the whale
swallowing Jonah. If God wants to do it, He will do it. If
God wants to fill a gas tank, He can do it. But when we
hear these stories, I wonder: Are we embellishing the truth
with the idea that the cause is good and there's a chance
that somebody will then be interested in accepting Christ?

Jesus does not need us to make Him look good. He *is*
good. He does not need an embellishment from any experience I may have had. Jesus is the Son of God; He was,
is, and always will be. Jesus stands on His own feet. He
does not need anything I can say to make Him anything
He is not already. We do not have to embellish the good
news of the gospel.

All Jesus calls us to do is to speak the truth. But we
often succumb to an easy lie. Maybe it is out of convenience, or out of cowardice, but often it is too easy to say
something that is not true—thinking it does not matter so
long as we are believed.

I am humiliated to say that has happened to me. Someone asked me a question and I knew the answer to her
question was not what she wanted to hear. But rather than
go into a long explanation, I simply said, "Yes." It was an
easy lie; but it was not easy, because God did not leave

me alone about it. I found myself having to go to that person and say, "Listen, what I said to you was not right." I had to humble myself and say, "Yes, I'm a preacher, but I responded to you incorrectly. I need to correct that."

I am convinced that I will never know a clear channel between myself and Christ if I allow those little foxes to spoil the vines and stay (Song of Solomon 2:15). I know we can be overly scrupulous about everything. But we are talking about honesty where we respond to a situation saying, "This is what it is." Maybe it's convenient to ignore the truth. Maybe it's cowardice that makes us say, "I don't want to face that." But whatever it is, the truth is always the better way.

Only One Way—Speak Truth

Critical to this ninth word is knowing that this simple truth is one of the most vital areas of human relationships and of human moral wellbeing. It is the concept of truth itself. We need a commitment to the truth whatever it may be, not allowing ourselves to be swayed by arguments, prejudices, or anything else we might wish.

God expects every one of us to be committed to the truth. We do not need to be afraid of the truth, because everything that is true is God's truth. Even if the theory of evolution were one day proven beyond a shadow of a doubt, I could accept that God was behind it, and therefore, I need not fear what this new understanding of our universe means for my faith.

God calls us to be bearers of truth. He expects us to seek out the truth in the answers we seek and the causes we serve. He expects us to respect the boundaries as they are honestly established in our relationships with one another.

There may be times when we have done or said something that's wrong and we have done nothing about correcting it. Sin never goes away except as we confess it and repent of it. We may be guilty at times of saying it doesn't matter if we tell a little "white lie." But if it matters enough for the Holy Spirit to impress upon our hearts that it is wrong, then there's only one thing to do. Confront, confess, repent of it, and find the peace that only God can give.

I did not find it pleasant to report the story about my wrong response to a question, but here's the rest of the story. As I prepared to preach, I knew there was no way I could stand in front of others and proclaim the gospel of truth while I accepted my own deviation from that truth.

Whether you stand to preach, or walk out into the world to live it, there is only one way to maintain truth. That is, not simply by saying it, but by living it.

Is the Holy Spirit speaking to your heart? Is there some issue you have shoved aside, and God has spoken to you, and you didn't think it necessary to respond? Is He still pressing you about it?

If God chooses to do that, you know it's important, because unless the channel is clear, the grace of God can never flow freely. Have you shared a juicy morsel that has struck a blow at someone else's character? Have you spoken something you know was not true and God has asked you to correct it? There is only one way to make it right— the way Christ has opened before us—the way of truth.

Chapter Nine Questions

Question: Has someone ever told a lie about you or to you? How did it impact your life? Have you ever told a lie about another person? What was the result in their life and in your own? Is there ever a time when it is biblically acceptable to tell a lie or "shade the truth"—why or why not?

_____

_____

_____

_____

_____

_____

_____

_____

Question: Are you quick to believe the worst, jump to conclusions, listen to gossip, or build prejudices? Do you share unverified information? What motivates your participation in gossip? How should a believer respond—what is the biblical process—when an accusation is brought against another person?

_____

_____

_____

_____

_____

_____

_____

_____

_____

_____

_____

Question: Do you ever exaggerate, elaborate, or embellish "for a good cause"? Do you ever lie by your silence, by not speaking the truth when it is needed? In what ways can you become a more truthful person? Ask the Holy Spirit to guide you and help you.

_____

_____

_____

_____

_____

_____

_____

_____

_____

_____

_____

Action: "You create something the moment you say something." How careful or careless is your speech? Have you used this power of creation in ways that build up or destroy? Read Matthew 12:36; Psalm 141:3; Proverbs 18:21; Ephesians 4:15, 4:25; and James 3:1–12. Choose at least one verse to memorize. How will you build habits of truthfulness and kindness into your speech?

Prayer: God, we pray that You would reinforce in our minds that this boundary is important. Truth is vital in our relationships to one another, to human society, and to our individual moral integrity. When we have compromised the truth and excused ourselves, saying it does not make any difference; when we have looked approvingly at someone we know has lied, may the Holy Spirit convict us of our own wrong. Help us, Lord Jesus, to confess, repent, and return to that place where You want us to be. We desire Your peace, available to us when we affirm the truth. We pray in Your name. Amen.

Chapter Nine Notes

_____

_____

_____

_____

_____

_____

_____

_____

_____

_____

_____

_____

_____

_____

_____

_____

_____

_____

CHAPTER TEN

The Tenth Word: Desire Good Things

You shall not covet your neighbor's house; you shall not covet your neighbor's wife, or his male servant, or his female servant, or his ox, or his donkey, or anything that is your neighbor's.

—*Exodus 20:17*

The Ten Commandments speak words of endearment for how the nation of Israel—and all of us—are to live. Throughout this book I've suggested that hardly anyone, religious or not, could read this list and not agree that we would have a wonderful world if everyone lived the way God called us.

And now we come to the last word—the tenth word—that says, "Do not covet your neighbor's wife, house, servants, livestock, or anything belonging to your neighbor." This is a unique word, this tenth word, as a subtle shift takes place here. Up to this point, God has been addressing specific actions: do not steal, do not commit adultery, do not lie. But now He speaks to something deeper than actions. He speaks to the attitude.

The idea of not coveting goes behind the actions to the desires of the individual and the choices being made. This commandment addresses the mind. It talks about our thoughts; it also addresses the affections. The word for *covet* in Hebrew means "desire."[55] This also addresses the will, because what we think about and desire goes forth into action by the choice of the will. So, what you have here is the first step to breaking the previous commandments. When does a person rob, kill, commit adultery, or lie? It's when one *covets* what belongs to another. In other words, another step has already been taken prior to those broken commandments, and it is the issue of *desire* God addresses in this word.

It would be interesting to notice how many times in Scripture this concept of wrong desire takes place. For example: In Genesis 3, Adam and Eve were in the garden; they knew God had set before them some wonderful gifts. They had numerous trees that bore delicious fruit. But there was one tree they were not to eat from—the tree of the knowledge of good and evil. But we find in Genesis 3:6 that Eve looked at this tree, desired its fruit, and she took it.

That pattern of looking longingly, then desiring and taking it, is a pattern you find on other occasions in Scripture. In fact, these same three words come up again in Joshua 7 when Achan went into Jericho. He disobeyed the ban placed on the booty, which God told the Israelites not to take. Achan took what was forbidden. When confronted, he said: when I saw, I desired, and I took (Joshua

7:20–21). This is the same pattern from Genesis 3. They saw, desired, and took.

There is the story of Ahab and Naboth in 1 Kings 21 regarding a piece of property owned by Naboth. Ahab, being the king, desired that choice piece of property. He desired it so fervently that finally his wife acted on his behalf. Naboth was falsely accused, falsely executed, and his property was taken by the king.

This is like the story of David and Bathsheba, isn't it (2 Samuel 11)? Bathsheba was Uriah's wife. But David was on top of his house one day and, as he looked out, he saw Bathsheba bathing. Rather than looking away, he looked further until he began to desire her. As a result, what David did was destructive, not only to Uriah, but it brought judgment upon David's life as well.

There is a Hebrew word for this, ḥemed, meaning "that which is desirable."[56] It is pleasant. As you look at this concept of the trees in the Garden of Eden, the trees were beautiful. The one in the center of the garden was the one that had such desirable-looking fruit, and Eve wanted it. But it was not only the fruit she wanted; she wanted to become as wise as God, knowing good and evil. It was that knowledge she desired most of all.

Whether we look at the Genesis account as an actual historical occurrence or simply a story explaining a concept (as some believe), the truth is there. In the middle of that garden God had given to Adam and Eve, there was the opportunity to exercise freedom, central to their bearing the image of God. If they were going to exercise dominion over creation, then God saw they needed the power of freedom, and He gave them that gift.

Why was *this tree* placed right in the center of the garden? Simply because it represented the central crux or decision of whether they would obey or disobey God. The issue was whether their freedom was going to be used in abuse of what God had given them, or whether they would yield themselves in subjection to God. The tree was desirable; it was pleasant. And the more Eve looked at it, the more she began to desire what it offered.

Examples from Other Religions

Many of the religions of the world recognize the role desire can have on our actions, and rather than teaching us to recognize and stay within the proper perspective of desire, they declare that what we need to do is exorcise from ourselves this desire. If we can get rid of desire, we can live the kind of life we should live.

One way to rid yourself of desire, according to some teachings, is through meditation. If we practice meditation, eventually we'll get to the point where we can separate our mind away from things and focus on the center of life, such as the divineness of every individual. You could escape the wheel and get right to the center where you lose desire.

The Stoics believed that the key to preventing desire from overtaking them was never to indulge in emotion. By separating themselves from emotion through pure reason, they could gain the highest and the best. In Paul's day, he confronted the Stoics (Acts 17:18–21).

Desire can be a dangerous thing. Some say we need to get away from all desire. They do it by meditation and escape, or they do it by separating themselves from it. In other words, the way I am going to achieve this kind of spirituality is to deny myself. I am going to deny the flesh. Even to this day some evangelical fundamentalists emphasize the idea that if we can deny our physical bodies, then we will achieve true spirituality.

That is not to say the practice of exercising power over your body is bad. There are times when we should separate ourselves from fleshly desires. But when the emphasis is on escaping desire by denying the body, there comes a point where you no longer have any kind of desire and instead you fall into a state of apathy.

There are those who simply flee from desire, such as the desert monks. Their way to get away from desire was to go into the desert alone, and there they could develop a holy life. But you see, the emphasis again is on fleeing, getting away from desire in order to be spiritual.

I knew a young married man in seminary who decided he would do as Jesus did and fast for forty days. He would take only liquids for the sustenance of his body. He talked to us about it afterward, and said he not only lost the desire for food, he also lost the desire for sex. So, if we separate ourselves by ascetic practices, we can triumph over desire. But is that all good?

Good Desire Versus Wrong Desire

As I look at all these beliefs, something needs to be answered. To desire or not to desire is *not* the question. Obviously, desire can lead us into terrible actions and sins. But there is a problem with trying to separate ourselves from everything that might tempt us and to lose all sense of desire. When God created the world, He made material things to be pleasant and desirable. The trees in the garden were all desirable. He said all of creation is *good*. The problem is not with desire itself, but rather with how we handle our desire.

The commandment does something else rather unique. You notice God said: Do not murder. Do not commit adultery. Do not steal. Do not lie. But He did not say, do not covet, and end it at that. God said do not *covet* your neighbor's house, wife, servants, and possessions. Do not desire these things. God did not say, "Do not desire anything."

The reason is that there is a place in Scripture for genuine and good desire. When Paul was talking to the Corinthians about spiritual gifts, he said, "But eagerly desire [covet] the higher gifts. And I will show you a still more excellent way" (1 Corinthians 12:31). It is the gift of love. Paul did not say, do not desire anything. He said we are to desire what is good.

I have listened numerous times to a recorded sermon by W. E. Sangster. The title of his message is "Covet Earnestly the Best Gifts,"[57] based on this verse at the close of 1 Corinthians 12. The point of his sermon is that desire can be good.

We should desire the greater gifts. We should desire to be conformed to the image of Jesus Christ (Romans 8:29). Again, to desire or not to desire is *not* the question. So, what is the question? It is obvious: Do we know the difference between wrong desires and right desires?

We confront the problem of wrong desires, because these separate us from God, leading us away from Him.

H. L. Ellison wrote that this sin "lies at the root of our social dissatisfaction and economic troubles."[58] It is an insult to God, "for he will not withhold any good gift." What Ellison means is that it is an insult to God to desire something someone else has, as though God's goodness and graciousness to you is not adequate. "It is not wanting more that is condemned, but wanting it at the expense of others." If I say I am longing for what is yours, I'm telling God that He has not provided adequately for me.

In addition, if we thought we would come face to face with a righteous judge, we would be more careful about the control of wrong desire. Psalm 10 is a beautiful psalm that addresses this issue in a few verses:

> For the wicked boasts of the desires of his soul, and the one greedy for gain curses and renounces the LORD. In the pride of his face the wicked does not seek him; all his thoughts are, "There is no God."
>
> —Psalm 10:3–4

And then at the end of this paragraph the psalmist stated: "The helpless are crushed, sink down, and fall by his might. He says in his heart, 'God has forgotten, he has hidden his face, he will never see it'" (Psalm 10:10–11).

Ellison also says that this wrong coveting, this wrong desire, is in total disregard of other people.[59] When I covet something that you possess, something that I may not have yet longed for, that longing is in disregard of you, your privileges, your rights, and your goods.

Wrong desires include the man who longs for his neighbor's wife or the woman who longs for her neighbor's husband. The ancient Israelite lived in disregard of the other person when he looked at the ox or the donkey belonging to the man next door and said, "I want those animals, I could use them and long to have them."

Accompanying that feeling of wanting what belongs to someone else is often the desire to take it away from that person. I want to have what belongs to you instead of celebrating the gifts you have been given. Therefore, I have no regard for you, or the blessings God has given you.

Wrong desire is always insatiable. It never brings happiness. You never satisfy wrong desire no matter how much you have. We received a letter from a friend about her visit to India. She had only one day to sightsee and went to the Taj Mahal. It was gorgeous, but that was not what occupied her mind. She had also seen the poverty of many people, and it was heart wrenching. That was the lasting impression from her trip. It was not the beauty of something manmade; it was the hunger and poverty of India's people.

Most of us in America are not going to bed hungry. We have heat for warmth, air conditioning for cooling, and a bed to sleep in. These comforts are accepted norms. Yet, we are not happy. We are living in a day when depression is running rampant among Americans. Our families are breaking up. We panic about what is taking place with our young people. We are fearful about where our nation is headed. We are not a happy people, yet we are a wealthy nation. Wrong desire has this problem: it is insatiable. Enough is not enough.

The person addicted to pornography will discover it is not enough to see one picture. It goes further and deeper.

Wrong desire wants more. The person who becomes addicted to drugs cannot use it once and stop. It goes further into a second step and a third step, until finally it consumes all of life. Wrong desire is never satisfied. As I look at Scripture, I understand why Paul wrote to the Christians in Rome:

> *What then shall we say? That the law is sin? By no means! Yet if it had not been for the law, I would not have known sin. For I would have not known what it is to covet if the law had not said, "You shall not covet."*
>
> *—Romans 7:7*

I think Paul focused on this one commandment against wrong desires as being the heart of the previous nine commandments. It is number ten because it sums up. I cannot say for certain, but I think Paul looked at himself, his need in life, and what he saw most was this idea of coveting. He recognized our desire for what does not belong to us when we are not living in correct alignment with God.

Matter of the Heart

Our entire relationship with God centers around the matter of the heart. The whole issue of a society not behaving as we ought lies in the matter of the heart. Jesus said in Matthew 15:19, "out of the heart come" the issues of life. God looks upon the heart, not only on our actions. We may pride ourselves that we have not robbed a bank or slandered a neighbor or committed adultery. But Scripture tells us that God looks upon our hearts. If I have

214 · DR. WILLIAM B. COKER, SR.

harbored wrong desires, these stand between me and God. In Harry Emerson Fosdick's book *The Meaning of Prayer*, he wrote that all real praying is a matter of desire.[60] God does not listen so much to the words as He reads the desire of the heart. Every prayer is a prayer of desire, and God knows our desires through our hearts. It is the dominant desire of the soul that God looks upon. Every person is a praying person, because prayer arises out of the desire of the heart. Do not covet. Do not harbor wrong desires. One day it will be the heart that God will judge.

How do we attack the problem of wrong desire? It is not enough to say it is a problem. How can we overcome and rise above the problem? If we are going to be conformed to the image of Christ, we must properly learn how to deal with the wrong desires in our heart.

Recognize the Problem of Wrong Desire

First, we must recognize the problem. Now, that may seem obvious. Most anyone addicted to a bad habit knows it is a problem. There's no other place the world beats up on us continuously or more consistently than at the place of wrong desire. The world is saying to us: "Here is something you need," or, "Here is something delightful."

For example, the problem of addiction to pornography is growing fast in our nation. So, what do the advertisers on television and other media use to appeal to us? Sex! Temptations abound. We find again and again the world is saying, here is something you need; it's delightful and desirable.

The serpent in the garden called Eve's attention to the tree. "This is one that will make you wise. This is what you need."

We recall the saying: *Necessity is the mother of invention.* There is a new one for Americans today: *Invention is the mother of necessity.* I've got to have that latest computer or automobile or gadget for the kitchen. For years we've lived without all these things, but now they've been invented, we have a sense of necessity. So, the problem in dealing with wrong desires is not only the attitudes inside us, it is also a continuous bombardment from outside.

Often wrong desires cover the real problem we must confront. People's attention may be directed to alcoholism or some other vice. The real problem is not our *sins*; it is to address the *sin* in the human heart. The atonement of Christ was not only meant to deal with our sin issues (the acts), but also the root of sin; it is then we will address the heart of the matter as the central problem.

The writer of Hebrews wrote that we are to "throw off everything that hinders and the sin that so easily entangles" (12:1 NIV). People want to look at this or that sin, but *the* sin is not some action we've done. Sin is about the fallenness of the human heart. Where I need the grace of God and what I need to address is my wrong "bent to sinning," as Charles Wesley stated in his hymn "Love Divine."[61] Address the sin problem in my life, not at these peripheral issues, but at the center, at the heart. I need to deal with wrong desire.

Attacking the Problem

Recognizing the problem of sin in the heart is the first place to deal with the problem of coveting. I believe three steps are workable in attacking the problem of wrong desire.

1. The first step is to make a commitment with our eyes. In Job 31:1, we find: "I made a covenant with my eyes not to look lustfully at a young woman" (NIV). Job was a married man, and he made a commitment with his eyes. Now, remember the pattern with Eve. She looked, she desired, and took. So, the place to address the problem is not at the took stage, it's at the look stage.

If I do not allow myself to look at things I know will lead me into wrong desires, I can separate myself from those things. Yes, I agree that is difficult in this world of bombardment. Sometimes, I can't help but see. But I can stop myself from looking *longingly*. To address the problem at the look stage, I can turn off the television program or internet video that is filled with vulgarity and sexual references. That is something you and I can do. So, where does it begin? It begins with a commitment to our eyes.

2. The second step is to make a commitment of our lives to the greater gifts God has given us. In Romans 12:21, Paul said we are to overcome evil with good. We're attacking the problem the wrong way when we try to get rid of desires, instead of putting desires in their proper place. If I am putting into place what's right and good, then there is no room for what's wrong and bad. If I do not make the room, there is no room. If I fill the house (and my head) with good desires, then there's no room for what's bad.

So, I commit my life to seek the higher gifts, to seek God's promises and seek to be conformed to the image of Christ. When issues arise, I have a higher desire.

That's the secret of a good marriage. People ask why marriages are breaking up. If both husband and wife commit themselves with a strong desire to making their marriage work, it will be done.

So, we make a commitment with our eyes, and we commit ourselves to higher desires by overcoming evil, not only with words but with good actions, because we want God to be at the center of our lives.

3. The third way to attack the problem is complete dependence on the Holy Spirit. As Christians, our primary dependence is on the work and power of the Holy Spirit. Jesus said to the disciples, do not leave Jerusalem "until you are clothed with power from on high" (Luke 24:49). I need the power of the Holy Spirit in order to be conformed to the image of Jesus Christ. That's what I need most, for if I am conformed to the image of Jesus Christ, then my life is a witness to the goodness of God for all the world to see.

I close with an emphasis on our children. We need to begin training our children, so they do not have wrong desires. If we wait until they are grown, their habits are set. I am firmly convinced that as parents, we should teach our children not only the difference between needs and wants, but that we can't always have what we want, and sometimes we don't get what we think we need. That is life. When we teach children that whatever they want they should get, we have set them on the course that is personally destructive.

There is no better place to begin this than at Christmas. It is amazing that every year some new doll is the trend, and parents are trying to get that new doll or toy for their child—whatever the cost. Most of our children have more things than they play with now. Yet, we keep buying them more. It is a wrong emphasis at Christmas to say to our children, whatever you want, make your list and Mom and Dad will get it for you. All we are doing is feeding the struggle they will one day have—to know the difference between good desires and wrong desires.

That is a hard step, isn't it? But it is needed.

Only the Beginning

As I said in the beginning, the last word serves as a capstone that holds all of the other commandments together. Our desires come from the focus of our heart. If our heart is focused on God and His will for our lives, then our desires are in correct alignment. But if our desires are focused on self, then we open ourselves up to all manner of sin whose ultimate consequences affect us and society.

Just as God's spoken word on the day of creation was only the beginning, God's spoken word to Israel on the mountain was the beginning of another sort—the beginning of an everlasting and transformational relationship with Him. As Jeremiah wrote:

Behold, the days are coming, declares the Lord, when I will make a new covenant with the house of Israel and the house of Judah, not like the covenant that I made with their fathers on the day when I took them by the hand to bring them out of the land of Egypt, my covenant that they broke, though I was their husband, declares the LORD. For this is the covenant that I will make with the house of Israel after those days, declares the LORD: I will put my law within them, and I will write it on their hearts. And I will be their God, and they shall be my people. And no longer shall each one teach his neighbor and each his brother, saying, "Know the LORD," for they shall all know me, from the least of them to the greatest, declares the LORD. For I will forgive their iniquity, and I will remember their sin no more.

—Jeremiah 31:31–34

God calls each of us into the same transformational relationship. In Christ, we are new creations (2 Corinthians 5:17) designed to live a holy life that seeks God's kingdom first, and in the process serve as guiding beacons of light to show the lost there is a better way to live.

Chapter Ten Questions

Question: How has chasing after the wrong desires caused you to break other commandments in your quest? Explain how obeying this final word will enable you to keep all the others.

_____

_____

_____

_____

_____

_____

_____

_____

_____

_____

Question: What do you most *desire* in your life? Are these desires good and healthy or wrong and sinful? How can wrong desires be yielded to God and transformed into godly desires? What should a Christian desire above all else, and how can you grow in these desires?

_____

_____

_____

_____

_____

_____

_____

_____

_____

_____

_____

Question: From pornography to Pinterest, what you *look at* can trigger wrong or selfish desires. How can you guard your heart from coveting by guarding your eyes? In what specific ways do you need to set up protection?

_____

_____

_____

_____

_____

_____

_____

_____

_____

_____

Action: How has God provided for you? How has God blessed you? Write down as long a list as you possibly can of the blessings that you enjoy, from everyday conveniences to material provision to educational or career opportunity to spiritual growth. Consider the things you covet in light of this list and spend some time in repentance and gratitude. Ask God to help you desire Him above any of His good gifts.

Prayer: Lord God, we pray that those desires that come into our hearts and minds may be distinguished by the truth of Your gospel. We know there are wrong desires, and we also recognize there are good desires. We know You want us to have those good desires; for You are not against pleasure. You are good. What You have warned us in these words is that we are to guard ourselves against those wrong desires that would harm us and our children. Teach us, Lord, we pray, to live in such a way that is conformable to the image of our Savior, Jesus Christ, in whose name we pray. Amen.

Chapter Ten Notes

CONCLUSION

Rightly Handling the Word of Truth

How do we handle God's Word correctly, in the right manner? We find the apostle Paul's answer in his second epistle to Timothy, chapter two, verses 8–15.

Remember Jesus Christ, risen from the dead, the offspring of David, as preached in my gospel, for which I am suffering, bound with chains as a criminal. But the word of God is not bound! Therefore I endure everything for the sake of the elect, that they also may obtain the salvation that is in Christ Jesus with eternal glory. The saying is trustworthy, for:

If we died with him, we will also live with him; if we endure, we will also reign with him; if we deny him, he also will deny us; if we are faithless, he remains faithful—for he cannot deny himself.

Remind them of these things, and charge them before God not to quarrel about words, which does no good, but only ruins the hearers. Do your best to present yourself to God as one approved, a worker who has no need to be ashamed, rightly handling the word of truth.

—2 Timothy 2:8–15

I've thought a great deal about this business of the gospel, particularly as I've come closer to the end of my ministry and have often evaluated what I've said or done. Along with studying various books on the subject, I've searched Scripture for what's important, what we often overlook. In Paul's letter to Timothy, we find several lessons.

In prison, bound with chains, Paul recognized life is short. Tradition tells us he was imprisoned for a period of time, was released, and later rearrested and returned to prison. At this point, he knew he was not going to be released a second time.

Paul knew what was ahead and he chose to write Timothy. In his letter, he reflected on his ministry, about what he had done and said. He thought about Timothy, this young man who was priceless to him in ministry, who joined and became part of the team who traveled around and shared the gospel of Christ. He gave Timothy instructions on how he needed to live, what he needed to do in ministry, but Paul also gave warnings, charging him to stay alert.

The Greek word Paul chose to use when giving his warning is translated from the Hebrew and is akin to one of the various words found in the Old Testament referring to God's Word. What Paul chose is the word meaning "testimonies," *diamartyromai*.[62] It has a sense of condemnation to it. It's the sense of being witnessed against. Indeed, as we see often in Scripture, God's Word is a witness against us when we're not doing what's needed. So, in his last words to Timothy, Paul gave him warnings, vital to remember when Paul would no longer be present to speak truth into his life.

Warnings

Paul first reminded Timothy of the centrality of Christ. Also, in First Corinthians, Paul gave a heavy emphasis on the centrality of Christ, for the center of our faith is not in ourselves. The center of our faith remains on Jesus Christ and Him crucified (1 Corinthians 2:2; 15:3). Christ is the focal point. He is the Word made flesh, the One we can see and know in terms of Scripture and walking with Him.

Although Paul was bound in prison and knew his time was short, he emphasized that the Word of God is not bound. We can bind people, but we cannot bind God's Word. That Word was lived out in a man like Paul. We don't have to wonder about Paul, for while he was in prison his life made an impact on those who gathered around him.

As we read the end of the book of Acts, Luke pointed out clearly that while Paul was in prison, he lived in such a way it affected the lives of his guards. (Acts 28:16–24.). Paul could say: "being chained like a criminal. But God's word is not chained" (2 Timothy 2:9 NIV). As Paul lived and shared his story, the Word of God touched the lives of other people.

Thus, Paul charged Timothy about some important personal responsibilities. He pointed out: "If we have died with him, we will also live with him; if we endure, we will also reign with him; if we deny him, he will also deny us; if we are faithless, he remains faithful, for he cannot deny himself. Remind them of these things, and charge them before God" (2 Timothy 2:11–14a). Paul urged Timothy to take up his responsibility.

There in verse 14, he again used a present imperative, which means, "Keep on doing this." He said to keep focused on Jesus, keep remembering Him, and keep reminding the people to whom you are ministering. That means a continuation, reinforcement, and reiteration of the message again and again and again.

In the process Timothy was also to remind them "not to quarrel about words" (2 Timothy 2:14b). How disastrous this has been, not only in church history, but even in the present day. Think of all the divisions that exist within Christendom—people who are divided along denominational titles or theological distinctions. We fight and quarrel over words, and while sometimes the words are significant, sometimes they are not. What I hear Paul saying to Timothy is: "Remember the focal point is still Christ."

In the community church I served, we had people from various backgrounds and denominations. We welcomed people into a church where we did not knock what other people thought or believed. We focused on Christ, because He is our primary purpose. Distinctions may be relevant to us, but that's not the major point. The major point is: God so loved the world that He gave His Son and He carried our sins on the cross that we might be reconciled with God. That is the primary focus we should all have.

We may differ about interpretations; we may differ about what words we use. But Paul said quarreling over words was useful for nothing. It doesn't accomplish anything.

When I first moved to a church I once pastored, a UPS man came and asked the secretary if I might be willing to debate his pastor. I told the secretary, "How would Jesus be honored by such a debate?" I'm not afraid to defend my position theologically, but what kind of a recommendation would that be to a broken world—two pastors battling each other over words and theological differences?

It's still "Christ and him crucified" (1 Corinthians 2:2), for He is the center of our faith. I'm not saying our theological views are not important. I am saying they are not the critical factor. The critical factor is Christ. To address this issue, Paul used a word translated "ruins":

*Remind them of these things, and charge them before God not to quarrel about words, which does no good, but only **ruins** the hearers.*
—2 Timothy 2:14 *(emphasis added)*

It's the same word from which we get *catastrophe*. In the Greek, it means "to turn upside down, to destroy, to ruin."[63]

When you're finished with the battle over differences, you have to ask, "Who won?" Everyone has been damaged and affected by it. We can say our side won, for we proved our point better, but we've left the church divided.

Personal Instructions

Paul then gave Timothy instructions for him personally. Paul charged him to strive earnestly, making every
effort to present himself before God with some lifestyle
objectives.

First, Timothy should present himself as one approved
(2 Timothy 2:15). And *dokimos*, the word used here, is
interesting, because in the verb form it's used for the
smelting of gold and the process of separation.[64] So the
word *dokimos* means you have been tested and you're approved.

Now in the book of Romans we find a negative form,
adokimos, and this is the person who was not proven.[65]
This is the person who has not stood the test and therefore
is reproved or debased. In the first chapter of Romans, we
see the stages of degradation as Paul told the people how
they drifted away from God further and further until they
ended up as "reprobate" (Romans 1:28 KJV). They are destroyed; they're broken. A catastrophe has taken place.
Paul said to Timothy: Labor to be tested and approved, not
ashamed, not disgraced by your life.

Some years ago, a pastor in Colorado was found to be
involved in homosexuality and drug use. One reporter
used the word "disgraced."[66] The tragedy is the pastor was
not the only one disgraced. He disgraced the Lord whom
he served. He disgraced the church he served. He disgraced everyone who pronounces the name of Christ as
Lord, because his actions were not hidden in a corner. Ask
yourself why every newspaper in the country carried the
story. It's another blow to the church and its message.

Paul urged Timothy to give careful attention to how he lived.

Lastly—and this is the phrase I wanted to grab onto—Paul wrote about "rightly handling the word of truth" (2 Timothy 2:15). Two Greek words are put together: *orthotomeō*.[67] The first is *orthos*, from which we get *orthodoxy*, the idea of being straight and right.[68] And then the word *temnō* means "to cut."[69] Combined, the word means "to cut straight through." It's used of cutting a straight road through a forest, for example. It's used only once, here in the New Testament, and twice in the Greek translation of the Old Testament, in Proverbs 3:6 and Proverbs 11:5. Proverbs 3:6 states: "In all your ways submit to him, and he will make your paths straight" (NIV). Acknowledge God and He will cut straight your path. That's the word.

So, Paul urged Timothy to cut or divide the Word straight and to handle the truth correctly.

Now I want to stop there, for I don't want to write about Timothy any longer. I want to address us, because often this business of dividing God's Word is done in such a way that we don't end up with truth. Instead, we hear what's contrary to the truth.

In English we have a word that uses the same idea. That's called *dichotomy*. It's been cut in two and usually has the sense of two things opposed to each other. When you say there's a dichotomy, things are not in agreement, but cut in two.

Paul is saying to Timothy: Be careful how you divide God's Word, for you don't want to create a false dichotomy by separating what cannot be separated. That's what I've been wrestling with for a long time, for it's been heavy on my mind. Therefore, what strikes me about dichotomies of today, in the sense of false cutting, is that we end up with what's opposed to each other. I examine with you three of my observations.

Law and Grace

Too often, people talk about the two words *law* and *grace* as though they are not harmonious terms. If you're going to talk about law, you can't mention grace; and if you talk about grace, you can't include law. In fact, people often make a division between the Old Testament and the New Testament, saying the Old Testament is all about law and the New Testament is all about grace. That's nonsense, because all you have to do is read the Old Testament. Yes, you'll find law there. God did give the Israelites the Law by which they could live, but the words of grace are there repeatedly. The Hebrew word *ḥesed*, translated "covenant love,"[70] is a word of grace, and the word *ḥēn* is the Hebrew word for *grace*.[71] The grace of God is seen all through the Old Testament.

When you come to the New Testament and say, "The New Testament is not about law, it's about grace," you've missed the point entirely. Why? Because of what Jesus said: "Do not think that I have come to abolish the Law or the Prophets; I have not come to abolish them but to fulfill them" (Matthew 5:17). He went on to say: "…not the least stroke of a pen, will by any means disappear from the Law until everything is accomplished" (Matthew 5:18 NIV).

The Law is the presentation of who God is—the character of God. As we've used the term, it's the moral photograph of God, His words of endearment. When we look at law and grace, there are people who say the Old Testament now is old fashioned and out of date, for now we're in New Testament times. In other words, we don't need the Old Testament anymore. People don't stop to realize the only way we can understand the New Testament is with the Old Testament.

If you only have the Old Testament, you're in Judaism where all of the promises, intents, and purposes of God have not yet been fulfilled. In the New Testament, Christ comes and fulfills the Law and at the same time shows us how to live in harmony with God. This idea of separating law and grace cannot exist.

Philip Bliss wrote a song titled, "Free from the Law, O Happy Condition."[72] The title of it really stunned me, because it stated we now are delivered from the Law. But the Law hasn't disappeared. We are still called to "love the Lord your God with all your heart and with all your soul and with all your mind" and to "love your neighbor as yourself" (Matthew 22:37, 22:39).

The Ten Commandments are still valid, at least in Christian circles. But the point Bliss was making is what Paul wrote in Galatians where he says the Law cannot redeem anybody. The Law can only condemn. And if you go only by the Law, you end up cursed (Galatians 3:13).

That makes perfect sense, because if I were to commit a crime today and got arrested, the law can convict me; it can condemn me; but the one thing it cannot do is deliver me. The law tells us where the boundary lines are drawn, where we understand God's Word and His will. It is like every athletic contest, for none of them make any sense unless boundaries are set. Those are laws. And every one of those is a negative. With a football game, the rules don't tell you the plays you can call. The rules tell you what you cannot do.

The Law remains, because God has set the moral boundaries for His people. If we accept those moral guidelines and walk in them, we please God. But if we violate the boundary, the Law can do absolutely nothing to change us. That was Paul's point. He said the only thing the Law has ever done for you is convict you. Is that bad? No. It's not any worse than having a law or a boundary set where you know how to deal with the game. God has set the boundaries for the game of life for us.

Those commandments He gave to the ancient Israelites, we still honor today. Imagine what would happen to us as a nation if everybody started obeying the social part of the commandments: not to rob, not to kill, not to commit adultery, not to lie, and not to covet. What a wonderful place this would be! If we could get to the place where we did not take what doesn't belong to us, if we did not kill one another, or abuse one another, it would be like heaven on earth, wouldn't it?

Can you imagine? No more locks on your doors. No worrying about your child playing out in front of the house. It would be marvelous. Whether we are religious or not, Christian or not, God's laws form the basis for a society that makes it possible to live together with respect. What we discover is that when we violate those principles, it makes it almost impossible to live with each other.

The Law is not something that's wrong. It's something that's right and good. Because without laws, where do we draw boundary lines? The problem comes when we incorrectly interpret what those boundaries are. As we look at Scripture, we understand law is important.

I love reading fantasy, and I've read a set called the *Duncton Chronicles* by William Horwood.[73] Of all things, the author wrote about moles. I've had those critters in my lawn, and I wish I could get rid of every one of them. But I enjoy reading these books because Horwood is not writing about moles, he's writing about people. In one book, the moles went through a terrible struggle. A new group came along, and they're the legalists. They make life miserable for themselves and everybody else.

Some say the Law can become disastrous. The legalists today are like the Pharisees who waited around ready to blast anyone who broke the Law. They were not happy themselves and made everyone else miserable.

Legalism, however, wasn't the problem in the early church. Their problem was antinomianism, the other extreme, where the Law was not important. They said: we're saved by grace; we don't have to follow those laws. We're redeemed; we can live like we want. In the early church, they battled with antinomianism, and we still struggle with it today, even in the church.

The Law is important, because it sets the pattern and shows us how we need to live. To separate law from grace is disastrous. Dietrich Bonhoeffer once said, "It is only when one submits to the law that one can speak of grace."[74] Until we understand the Law and how we have violated the Law, we cannot talk about grace. It's meaningless.

The Law condemns because it shines a light on where we fall short. Grace covers us, offering us the opportunity to begin again and to allow God to transform our lives from the inside out. And God, in His infinite wisdom, has given us both.

Faith and Works

A second dichotomy is between faith and works. On this point, Martin Luther did no favors to Protestants. He looked at the epistle of James and said it's an "epistle of straw."[75] Why? Because it was about works. James wrote that if you don't have works, you don't have faith. Luther had come out of the background of salvation by works, and so James' teaching was anathema to Luther. For him, the idea of works and faith were separated. We hear people say, I am saved by grace through faith. Praise the Lord! That's scriptural. Does that mean works are now inconsequential to us? Not in the least!

Here's a definition, by pastor Harry Emerson Fosdick, I've quoted many times: "Faith is holding reasonable convictions, in realms beyond the reach of final demonstration."[76] You can't prove faith, because if you could, you wouldn't have faith; you would have facts. Faith is something you can't finally demonstrate. For one reason, we can't bring God down and set Him on display and say, "See, here's God." There are reasonable convictions; yet they're beyond the reach of final demonstration. That's faith. But what else does Fosdick add in his definition? He said: "…and, as well, it is the thrusting out of one's life upon those convictions as though they were surely true."[77] There is no separation at this point, because works manifest our faith.

What we do is a revelation of what we think and what we believe. We can apply it in every area of our lives. Sometimes, we do silly or stupid things, but basically we don't go around living in a way that's contrary to what we believe.

I can think of multitudes of illustrations to fit. If I told you it was dangerous to walk across a certain bridge and you believed it, are you going to take off across the bridge? No, you'd say, I'm not going to do that because it's dangerous. What you think affects what you do.

When we come to the Christian gospel and read what Paul and the other apostles have conveyed, we notice they've said you can talk about faith, and by that you understand your life, its meaning and purpose, its beginning and ending. You cannot say, "this is my belief, my conviction, my faith," and then proceed to go out into your daily routines and live in a way that's totally contradictory.

Why was the pastor in Colorado condemned? Because he did something no other human being has done? No. Why? Because his life did not reflect what he claimed to believe. Everything he preached on Sunday was contradicted by his liaisons with homosexuality and drug use. Look how the newspapers picked up on that.

You cannot divide works and faith. It isn't that we're saved by the works we do. It is because we act upon what we believe, and we know it is by grace through faith that Christ touches and changes our lives.

My life was changed, not by something I accomplished, but because I discovered God loves me and He sent His Son for my sake, for my redemption. Every area of my life comes under the scrutiny of what I believe. If I claim to be a follower of Christ, the world has every right to hold me to what I say and every right to criticize what I do when it is contrary to what I say.

The greatest problem we face in the church in America today is our inconsistency between what we do on Sunday morning and what we do Monday morning through Saturday night.

Harry Blamires, a British author, wrote *The Christian Mind*.[78] I had the privilege of meeting him when he came to Asbury College where I was teaching, and we talked about his book. He told me that he had observed conversations among people, those who make the profession of believing in Christ. When he listened to them in outside groups, they didn't talk any differently than other people do. Their ideas, the things they talk about, were no different. His point was: How can we talk about Christ in our lives and yet it makes no difference how we live?

That's why this has weighed heavily upon my mind, not only about my personal life, but what is also true of the church at large. We never will have a message to bear rightly if our lives are contradictions of the gospel we talk about on Sunday morning. Faith and works are indivisible. They're stuck together. It is "the thrusting out of one's life on those convictions as though they're surely true."[79]

Secular and Religious

The third dichotomy is: we can't divide the secular world from the religious world. There's no way, as Christians, we cannot take faith into our secular lives, because it overlaps. We see it time and again. Our faith needs to operate in every area of life.

Andrew Kirk wrote a book titled, *God's Word for a Complex World*.[80] The thrust of his book was more politically oriented than it was trying to explain spiritually some passages of Scripture. His focus, though, went back to the Old Testament, and what he discovered was that God's interest in His people was not centered on what they did in the temple at certain times. The emphasis was on what they did in their secular lives, where they dealt with the question of how to structure the nation and how to relate with one another.

In the Jubilee Year, the fiftieth-year celebration in ancient Israel, every slave was set free, and every piece of property returned to its original owner (Leviticus 25). No individual lost his property. Why did God institute this practice? Did it have anything to do with salvation? No. It came down to how we deal with people and how we relate to one another. God drilled into the ancient Israelites: "I am not interested in your worship of Me unless it spills over into how you act with one another. How do you deal with the brother who has been sold into slavery or the person who has lost his property because of financial failure and difficulties?"

Through the prophets, God said to His people: "I'm sick and tired of your worship. I don't want to hear your songs anymore. I don't want to smell your sacrifices anymore. Your offerings are useless. They mean nothing whatsoever. I asked you to live your lives in righteousness, yet there is no discernable difference in your lives compared to the lives of those who are worshiping false gods."

More than our worship, how we practice justice with one another is what interests God. Righteous behavior belongs in our personal and public lives. The Old Testament is replete with these constant references to the social and political. As God moved in the nation of Israel, He spoke about the people's offerings and about the responsibilities of the king. God laid out a plan, because they were to understand their relationship to Him could not be separated from their relationship to one another. We find this emphasis in the Ten Commandments.

We hear much today about the Constitution and the "separation of church and state." That was never the intent of the First Amendment. It never said there should be a wall of separation between what a person believes and what we do in our government. What it did say is the government could not establish a religion. When Thomas Jefferson wrote to the church in Virginia and used the phrase about the wall of separation, this was in response to their request for the President of the United States to declare Thanksgiving a national holiday.[81] He answered them, in effect: "I'm sorry, that's not the function of the federal government; that's your function."

The state does not establish religion. Never did. The First Amendment did suggest we could have a state in which our religious faith could be expressed. As one writer said, there is no barbed-wire fence between inner and outer reality. You cannot separate what you believe from what you do.

As Christians, we must model what we claim the gospel is all about, for we live in a way to bring glory to God.

This follows the rules God has set before us in the Decalogue and throughout the rest of Scripture.

I cannot separate my faith from what I do, and neither can you. I tell you again, what is killing the church today is the inconsistency between what we say and what we do.

Closing Prayer

Father, we pray because every one of us wrestles with the question of how we live out our faith, given the world around us, which is not a friend to grace. How do we meet the challenges that come up about voting and about being involved in social issues? It's much more. It's about our attitudes, about the many decisions we encounter. It's about what we say to people. How far do we compromise ourselves in order to be accepted? Do we stand up to be counted in spite of the fact everybody else may disagree?

Father, we thank You for Your Word. Help us to understand it's not only about having worship services. Your Word is about living our lives day by day according to what You have shown us about ourselves, about You, and about Your purpose and Your will. Father, we need help, and we thank You for the Holy Spirit who is faithful to us. Amen.

The Mirror Test

I believe truth is applicable to all of life and not only to our spiritual life. I want to ask you some tough questions. Take a moment to think before you answer these simple yet important questions.

Question: In my daily living, do I exalt laws so as to be called a legalist, or do I lean more on grace and ignore obedience to God's moral law? What can I do to find the balance?

_____

_____

_____

_____

_____

_____

_____

_____

_____

_____

_____

Question: Is there any inconsistency between my Christian profession and how I live my daily life?

_____

_____

_____

_____

_____

_____

_____

_____

_____

_____

_____

Question: Is there a place where my actions are undermining my confession of faith?

_____

_____

_____

_____

_____

_____

_____

_____

_____

Question: Is it possible others don't pay attention to my spiritual life because of my social life? Is my life in the midst of community a contradiction to the boundaries the Lord has set in place?

_____

_____

_____

_____

_____

_____

_____

_____

REFERENCES

Notes

1. *Lexico,* "endearment." https://www.lexico.com/en/definition/end earment.

2. *Online Etymology Dictionary,* "endearment." https://www.etymon line.com/word/endearment.

3. Buber, Martin. "What Are We to Do About the Ten Commandments? Reply to an Inquiry." 1929. In *The Martin Buber Reader*, edited by A. D. Biemann. Palgrave Macmillan, New York, 2002. https://link.springer.com/chapter/10.1007/978-1-137-07671-7_4.

4. *Blue Letter Bible,* "Strong's H4687: *mitsvah*." https://www.blueletterbible.org/lang/Lexicon/Lexicon.cfm?strongs=H4687&t=KJV.

5. Kaufmann, Yehezkel. *The Religion of Israel.* University of Chicago Press, 1960.

6. Strong, James. "H8552: *tāmam.*" *Strong's Exhaustive Concordance of the Bible.* Zondervan, 2001.

7. Church of England. *The Book of Common Prayer, and Administration of the Sacraments, Together with the Psalter.* John Baskett, 1737.

8. Palmer, G. E. H. *The Philokalia.* Vol. 2. Faber & Faber, 2011, p. 507.

9. Davidman, Joy. *Smoke on the Mountain: An Interpretation of the Ten Commandments.* Westminster Press, 1954, p. 21.

10. Davidman, *Smoke on the Mountain,* p. 21.

11. Varughese, T. V. "Christianity and Technological Advance—the Astonishing Connection." *Institute for Creation Research,* November 1, 1993. https://www.icr.org/article/christianity-technological-advance-astonishing-con/.

12. Lewis, C. S. *The Lion, the Witch, and the Wardrobe.* © CS Lewis Pte Ltd 1950. Used with permission.

13. Busman, Joshua. "Exercising Your Second Commandment Rights: Luther and Calvin on Music." *The Other Journal: An Intersection of Theology and Culture,* May 18, 2012. https://theotherjournal.com/2012/05/18/exercising-your-second-commandment-rights-luther-and-calvin-on-music/.

14. Albright, William F. *From the Stone Age to Christianity: Monotheism and the Historical Process.* John Hopkins Press, 1946.

15. Phillips, J. B. *Your God Is Too Small.* Touchstone, 2004.

16. Gabler, Neal. *Life: The Movie: How Entertainment Conquered Reality.* Vintage, 2000.

17. *Biblical Name Vault,* "Methuselah." Abarim Publications. http://www.abarim-publications.com/Meaning/Methuselah.html#.XfAhsC2ZMW8.

18. Shakespeare, William. *Othello* 3.3.198–203. Harvard University, 1905, p. 67–68.

19. Benner, Jeff A. "The Ten Commandments in Ancient Hebrew." Ancient Hebrew Research Center. https://www.ancient-hebrew.org/biblical-history/ten-commandments-in-hebrew.htm.

20. *Merriam-Webster,* "vain." https://www.merriam-webster.com/dictionary/vain.

21. Strong, James. "H5375: *nāśā'.*" *Strong's Exhaustive Concordance of the Bible.* Zondervan, 2001.

22. Hamilton, Victor P. "2338a." *Theological Wordbook of the Old Testament.* Vol. 2. Edited by R. Laird Harris, Gleason L. Archer, Jr., and Bruce K. Waltke. Moody Press, 1980.

23. Browning, Robert. "Rabbi Ben Ezra," line 2. T. Y. Crowell, 1902.

24. Lewis, C. S. *The Last Battle*. Scholastic, 1995, p. 203. © CS Lewis Pte. Ltd 1956. Used with permission.

25. God actively engaged with the Israelites through the stories of their patriarchs. For further discussion of these concepts, see Abraham Joshua Heschel's *The Sabbath: Its Meaning for Modern Man* (1951) and *Between God and Man: An Interpretation of Judaism*, edited by Fritz A. Rothschild (1959).

26. Strong, James. "H7673: *šābat*." *Strong's Exhaustive Concordance of the Bible*. Zondervan, 2001.

27. Laband, David N., and Deborah Hendry Heinbuch. *Blue Laws: The History, Economics, and Politics of Sunday-Closing Laws*. Lexington Books, 1987.

28. Hirsch, Emil G., Joseph Jacobs, and Julius H. Greenstone. "Sabbath." *Jewish Encyclopedia*. http://www.jewishencyclopedia. com/articles/12962-sabbath.

29. Strong, James. "H3513: *kābēd*." *Strong's Exhaustive Concordance of the Bible*. Zondervan, 2001.

30. Strong, James. "H3516: *kābēd*." *Strong's Exhaustive Concordance of the Bible*. Zondervan, 2001. See also "H3515: *kābēd*."

31. Strong, James. "H3513: *kābēd*." *Strong's Exhaustive Concordance of the Bible*. Zondervan, 2001.

32. Davidman, *Smoke on the Mountain*, p. 61.

33. Stott, John. *Between Two Worlds*. Wm. B. Eerdmans Publishing Co., 2017.

34. Bush, George W. "President Bush's Last Televised Address." *The New York Times*. January 15, 2009. https://www.nytimes.com/ 2009/01/15/us/politics/15bush-text.html?pagewanted=all&_r=0.

35. Strong, James. "H7523: *rāṣaḥ*." *Strong's Exhaustive Concordance of the Bible*. Zondervan, 2001.

36. Strong, James. "G2839: *koinos*." *Strong's Exhaustive Concordance of the Bible*. Zondervan, 2001.

37. U. S. Food and Drug Administration. "Tabacco: Importing and Exporting." https://www.fda.gov/tobacco-products/products-guidanc e-regulations/importing-and-exporting.

38. Landman, Anne. "Philip Morris Pushing Smoking Hard in

Foreign Countries." Center for Media and Democracy PRWatch, 2010. https://www.prwatch.org/news/2010/03/8928/philip-morris-pushing-smoking-hard-foreign-countries.

39. Ellison, H. L. *Exodus*. Daily Study Bible Series. Westminster John Knox Press, 1982, p. 113.

40. Singer, Peter. "Taking Life: Humans." *Practical Ethics*. 2nd edition. Cambridge University Press, 1993, p. 175–217. https://www.utilitarian.net/singer/by/1993----.htm.

41. Fosdick, Harry Emerson. "God of Grace and God of Glory." 1930. In Hymnary.org. https://hymnary.org/text/god_of_grace_and_god_of_glory.

42. National Right to Life. "Abortion Statistics: United States Data and Trends." https://nrlc.org/uploads/factsheets/FS01Abortioninthe US.pdf.

43. Finer, L. B., and S. K. Henshaw. "Abortion Incidence and Services in the United States in 2000." *Perspectives on Sexual and Reproductive Health* 25, no. 1 (2003). p. 6–15.

44. British Board of Film Classification. "Children See Pornography As Young As Seven, New Report Finds." September 26, 2019. https://bbfc.co.uk/about-bbfc/media-centre/children-see-pornography-young-seven-new-report-finds.

45. Lewis, C. S. *Mere Christianity*. HarperCollins, 1980, p. 106.

46. Peck, M. Scott. *The Road Less Travelled: A New Psychology of Love, Traditional Values and Spiritual Growth*. Arrow, 1996.

47. Shakespeare. *Othello* 3.3.198–203.

48. Charlton, Thomas Usher Pulaski. *The Life of Major General James Jackson*. N.p., 1809, p. 85.

49. Emerson, Ralph Waldo. "Human Culture: Being and Seeming." *The Early Lectures of Ralph Waldo Emerson*. Vol. 2. Edited by Robert E. Spiller and Stephen E. Whitcher. Harvard University Press, 1964, p. 318.

50. Strong, James. "H6030: *ānâ*." *Strong's Exhaustive Concordance of the Bible*. Zondervan, 2001.

51. Strong, James. "H7723: *shaw*." *Strong's Exhaustive Concordance of the Bible*. Zondervan, 2001.

52. Emerson, "Human Culture," p. 318.

53. Strong, James. "H1697: *dabâr.*" *Strong's Exhaustive Concordance of the Bible.* Zondervan, 2001.

54. Strong, James. "H1696: *dabar.*" *Strong's Exhaustive Concordance of the Bible.* Zondervan, 2001.

55. Strong, James. "H2530: *chāmad.*" *Strong's Exhaustive Concordance of the Bible.* Zondervan, 2001.

56. Strong, James. "H2531: *hemed.*" *Strong's Exhaustive Concordance of the Bible.* Zondervan, 2001.

57. Sangster, W. E. "Covet Earnestly the Best Gifts." Recorded message from service at Asbury Theological Seminary.

58. Ellison, *Exodus,* p. 115.

59. Ellison, *Exodus,* p. 115.

60. Fosdick, Harry Emerson. "Prayer As Dominant Desire." Chap. 8 in *The Meaning of Prayer.* Pilgrim Press, 1915, p. 133–151.

61. Wesley, Charles. "Love Divine, All Loves Excelling." Public domain, 1747. In Hymnary.org. https://hymnary.org/text/love_divine_all_love_excelling_joy_of_he.

62. Strong, James. "G1263: *diamartyromai.*" *Strong's Exhaustive Concordance of the Bible.* Zondervan, 2001.

63. Strong, James. "G2692: *katastrŏphē.*" *Strong's Exhaustive Concordance of the Bible.* Zondervan, 2001.

64. Strong, James. "G1384: *dokimos.*" *Strong's Exhaustive Concordance of the Bible.* Zondervan, 2001.

65. Strong, James. "G96: *adokimos.*" *Strong's Exhaustive Concordance of the Bible.* Zondervan, 2001.

66. CNN. "Disgraced Pastor Haggard Admits Second Relationship with Man." https://www.cnn.com/2009/US/01/29/lkl.ted.haggard/.

67 Strong, James. "G3718: *orthotomeō.*" *Strong's Exhaustive Concordance of the Bible.* Zondervan, 2001.

68. Strong, James. "G3717: *orthos.*" *Strong's Exhaustive Concordance of the Bible.* Zondervan, 2001.

69. Strong, James. "G5114: *temnō.*" *Strong's Exhaustive Concordance of the Bible.* Zondervan, 2001.

70. Strong, James. "H2617: *hesed.*" *Strong's Exhaustive*

Concordance of the Bible. Zondervan, 2001.

71. Strong, James. "H2580: *ḥēn*." *Strong's Exhaustive Concordance of the Bible.* Zondervan, 2001.

72. Bliss, Philip. "Free from the Law, O Happy Condition." Public domain. In Hymnary.org. https://hymnary.org/text/free_from_the_law_o_happy_condition.

73. Horwood, William. *Duncton Wood.* McGraw-Hill Education, 1980.

74. Bonhoeffer, Dietrich. Quoted in John D. Godsey, *The Theology of Dietrich Bonhoeffer.* Wipf and Stock, 2015, p. 277.

75. Luther, Martin. *Prefaces to the New Testament.* Translated by E. Theodore Bachmann and Charles M. Jacobs. Wildside Press, 2010, p. 10.

76. Fosdick, Harry Emerson. *The Meaning of Faith.* Abingdon Press, 1917, p. 12.

77. Fosdick, *The Meaning of Faith.*

78. Blamires, Harry. *The Christian Mind: How Should a Christian Think?* Regent College, 2005.

79. Fosdick, *The Meaning of Faith.*

80. Kirk, Andrew. *God's Word for a Complex World.* Zondervan, 1987.

81. Rasmussen, Frederick N. "Not All Presidents Officially Called for Thanksgiving." *The Baltimore Sun.* November 29, 2009. https://www.baltimoresun.com/news/bs-xpm-2009-11-29-0911280034-story.html.

About the Author

A native of New Orleans, Dr. William B. Coker Sr. graduated from Tulane University in 1957. Answering the call to preach, Bill pastored churches in Louisiana, Mississippi, Kentucky, and Indiana. Committed to the truth, Bill finished graduate programs at Asbury Theological Seminary (B.D. and Th.M.) and Hebrew Union College (Ph.D.). He served as assistant professor at ATS and then as professor of Bible and Greek at Asbury College (University), along with two terms as Vice President of Academic Affairs. For two years Bill was Vice President for Mission Advancement at OMS International (One Mission Society). His last pastorate was World Gospel Church, Terre Haute, Indiana (1989–2008), and while there he worked on many teams with the Emmaus El

Shaddai community. After retirement, Bill assisted the senior pastor of Free Life Community Church in Terre Haute.

Bill and his wife, Ann L. Coker, now live in Indianapolis, Indiana, where they attend Southport Presbyterian Church. They have four grown children, ten grandchildren, and twelve great-grandchildren. Ann graduated from Asbury College (University) 20 years after completing high school. She worked as managing editor of *Good News* magazine, and she contributed to *The Woman's Study Bible*, NKJV, Thomas Nelson Publishers. She writes for devotional publications, periodicals, and her blog (www.abcoker.blog). She has served the pro-life cause in several agencies. Ann is a member of Heartland Christian Writers in Indianapolis.